I MARRIED A MYSTIC

Kirsten Buxton

I Married a Mystic
by Kirsten Buxton
ISBN: 978-1-942253-27-3

First Printed Edition 2016

Living Miracles Publications
P.O. Box 789, Kamas, UT 84036 USA
publishing@livingmiraclescenter.org
+1 435.200.4076

LIVING MIRACLES

This book was joyfully produced by the Living Miracles Community
—a non-profit ministry run by inspired modern-day mystics
devoted to awakening.

Editor's Notes:

- Kirsten often gives voice to thoughts within the mind. These thoughts are presented in italics rather than within quotation marks.

- The words "the Course" and the acronym ACIM are used interchangeably throughout this book to refer to *A Course in Miracles*.

- Kirsten's actions or internal notes during the journaling with the Holy Spirit are inside square brackets.

Bibliography

All quoted material from *A Course in Miracles*© (Third Edition, 2007) is used with written permission granted by The Foundation for Inner Peace, publisher and copyright holder. (PO Box 598, Mill Valley, CA 94942, USA - www.acim.org and info@acim.org).

A Course in Miracles quotes are referenced using the following system:
T: Text
W: Workbook for Students
M: Manual for Teachers

Example:
"All real pleasure comes from doing God's Will." T-1.VII.1
T-1.VII.1 = Text, Chapter 1, Section VII, paragraph 1

Kirsten Buxton

Kirsten Buxton has devoted her life to living and demonstrating the teachings of *A Course in Miracles*. She experiences life as an ebb and flow of inspiring collaborations and inward mystical phases. Kirsten is delighted to be an instrument for the Spirit's expression of love through inspiring projects, including; overseeing spiritual centers, counseling, and teaching extensively throughout the world. She has also co-developed a multimedia mind training and ministerial program, written songs, performed at music concerts, recorded albums and produced meditation apps and CDs. Her authentic approach to awakening has resulted in a deep, unshakable trust and awareness of the Spirit—this is the gift she offers to everyone she meets. She continues to share her experiences and insights through movie reviews, music, and other writings on her website.

Kirsten lives in spiritual community with David Hoffmeister and other mighty companions devoted to awakening.

Foreword

Deep inside, everyone longs for union, connection, and love. The calling of the heart is for continuity, and an abiding feeling of closeness. The journey to God is the reawakening of the soul, and the sojourn from human love to the oneness of heaven. With God all things are possible, and it is a delight to watch a little willingness given to the spirit transform the mind and result in a forgiven world.

Kirsten and I came together to experience a love that never ends. Our relationship and marriage was given over to the spirit as a means of spiritual awakening, through forgiveness. This holy relationship was our means of turning inward, releasing all thoughts of the past, and all ambitions for the future, to bask content in the present moment. Kirsten recorded the narrative of our lives as a rare glimpse of an accelerated, and often intense, pathway to a love not of this world.

It is the prayer of my heart that this story will bless those who yearn for forgiveness and the remembrance of God's Love. May our experiences speed you along the way that is given, that you may embrace the glad tidings of forgiveness, and experience true love and joy. Our song of gratitude to Jesus and the Holy Spirit is expressed through these pages—touched by the One Who created us whole and complete in love.

Forever in love,
David Hoffmeister

Table of Contents

Preface

Born and raised in rural New Zealand, and highly independent from the moment she could walk, Kirsten assumed responsibility for saving the world at a young age. At thirteen, after years as an environmental activist, Kirsten felt depressed and unable to fix or change the world. She gave up and turned to drugs and alcohol as a way to cope.

Kirsten dropped out of school and rebelled, but this didn't bring her the freedom she was seeking. Later, she turned towards a career in education in the hope of finding a solution there.

As a young adult, Kirsten felt a calling that she couldn't put into words. She knew that settling down and leading a normal life would not be enough for her, and she bought a one-way ticket to Europe. Backpacking through many countries where she didn't speak the language forced her to rely solely on her intuition as her guide. This fulfilled something within her that she had longed for, and practicing yoga and dance opened her mind to a whole new world of spirituality.

After years of these transformative experiences living abroad, the time came when Kirsten reluctantly returned to New Zealand. Afraid that her expansion could come to a halt, disillusionment and restlessness soon set in. She filled each moment with activity; a new career, friends, mountain biking, and skiing.

Two years later, Kirsten was inwardly exhausted, yet felt unable to stop. She prayed for help. Alone in the forest she fell from her mountain bike, and life as she knew it came to an end. She was twenty-seven years old. The accident resulted in two broken wrists and a brain injury, chronic fatigue, and migraines. She could no longer manage her own life.

Kirsten's accident launched her on a journey of healing through a range of modalities, culminating in a devoted meditation practice of up to eight hours a day. She fell in love with the profound peace that she experienced during meditation, and she soon knew that this presence of peace was the only thing she truly wanted. Her spiritual journey had begun in earnest.

During meditation Jesus unexpectedly appeared to Kirsten saying, "From now on, I will be your guide." He said that if she continued to do things her way, she would not heal. However, old habits die hard, and the old pattern of pushing herself resulted in another serious sporting accident.

This hit her hard psychologically as she knew she was in danger of killing herself. She fell to her knees and cried out for help. What followed was a revelatory experience—an experience of such intense Divine Love that she immediately gave her life over to God.

Shortly afterwards, Kirsten was given the book *A Course in Miracles* (ACIM). Upon opening the book and reading, "... you have no control over the world you made" she had an epiphany—she had always tried to manage her life and her world! T-12.III.9 She knew immediately that this book was the answer to the prayer of her heart, and that she would need to relinquish all control over her life in order to heal.

Kirsten found studying *A Course in Miracles* to be pure nourishment for her soul. She felt as though Jesus had written each daily Workbook Lesson just for her—as if the ink was still wet on the page. Her life now took on a profound sense of purpose that was rooted in the present moment, and she experienced for the first time that she was not dependent on the world for her happiness.

Kirsten had many questions about the nature of life, love, relationships, and truth, and she knew that her work with the Course would reveal the answers. She had no idea what the future held, but for the first time in her life she wasn't afraid of the unknown. What came next was beyond anything Kirsten could have ever imagined!

Sinking into Silence
Deeper and deeper,
Enfolded in Your everlasting peace,
Deepening, deepening, ever deepening,
Into You, I Am …

Presence, Peace
Divine Silence welcomes Allness,
Being … Home
Words dissolve
The world has gone

Deeper and deeper into Silence I come
You called, I called,
You heard, I came
United in Love, We are.

Chapter One
Meeting a Mystic

Spring/Summer/Fall/Winter 2004

"This world you seem to live in is not home to you. And somewhere in your mind you know that this is true. A memory of home keeps haunting you, as if there were a place that called you to return, although you do not recognize the voice, nor what it is the voice reminds you of." W-182.1

Surrender

I fell to my knees and cried out for help. I'd been knocked unconscious twice within eighteen months, and both "accidents" had happened just as I'd had the thought, "I don't want to be here." I knew that if I didn't give my life over completely, I was going to kill myself. Literally.

What happened next changed my life completely. I had a direct experience of God's Love that is almost impossible to convey. What I can say, is that on my knees I found myself shaking and crying, feeling an indescribable love radiating throughout my entire being. It was unlike anything I had experienced before and had nothing to do with anything of this world. It was so whole and pure, deep, and breathtaking, that my life was changed forever.

I knew that I was loved beyond anything I had ever understood. I knew that this love, this huge presence of majesty and grace, was behind everything, aware of everything, loving me always. In this recognition, my life was given over. Never again could I pretend to know my own best interests unless I was in direct contact with this awareness. I felt, for the first time in my life, that I could relax and trust that the Spirit was in charge.

The Journey Begins

Seven months later I was invited to dinner to meet David Hoffmeister, an American mystic. I had never met David and knew almost nothing about him. Recently I had watched him on a DVD where he was walking into a canyon, talking about the present moment. He was a vibrant, blue-eyed man in his forties; he appeared very peaceful and happy, as if he were having a mystical experience.

As I was getting ready, I felt butterflies in my stomach, as if I were going on a date. How surprising! Suddenly I remembered that whilst watching David on the DVD, I'd heard the Spirit say, "This is your life partner!" *What is happening?* I wondered. I didn't know what to make of this, and I didn't dare tell anyone. I was so shocked at the enormity and unexpectedness of this message that I had pushed it out of awareness immediately.

At dinner that night were my parents, Jackie and Roger, and their friends, Mia and Lars, and David and I. Jackie and Mia had been *A Course in Miracles* (ACIM) students for two years and had gone as far as they could with their current study group and had searched online for someone who was living the Course. They were thrilled when they found David and he accepted their invitation to come to New Zealand.

The night was so much fun. Roger and Lars, Jackie's and Mia's husbands, took turns making light of the few Course principles they had picked up, making sure we were all well aware that *they* were the ones who had provided the credit card for David's plane ticket and the meal—not God. Jackie and Mia had their hands full trying to redirect the conversation back to sincere spiritual questioning. I watched as David had a wonderful time, his blue eyes sparkling with delight. It seemed that he had nothing to prove, and his humble presence and graciousness were compelling. His joyful Spirit could handle anything from any angle, and use it as a means to connect. From motorbikes and tennis, to private thoughts and husband and wife dynamics, it all became a swirling, joyous conversation.

A Surprising New Direction

Two days after dinner, Jackie and I drove to Mia's house for a weekend retreat with David. I went to my room to settle in and sat on my bed to meditate. David walked past my room, appearing so ordinary, in his shorts, sandals and polo shirt. He felt like a big, soft, presence of love. I found myself inviting him to join me. "I'd love to!" he replied, and together we sank into a beautiful, peaceful meditation.

The Spirit poured through David as he spoke that night and throughout the weekend. As I was still recovering from two head injuries, I often had my eyes closed as I listened. At times I curled up on the floor on some cushions. It was a miracle that I could stay in the gatherings all day since my energy levels were usually exhausted by early afternoon. But in this gentle, vibrant energy of the Spirit I felt nourished by every word that David spoke. This felt very deep for me. I realized that most of the exhaustion I usually felt was actually because I was tired of the world; I could only handle being aware of it for so long. But when listening to David, I felt that what was coming towards me was loving and supportive for my mind and soul. For the first time in eighteen months I had real hope that the head injury symptoms that seemed to dominate my life were temporary. I knew that this shift was directly connected to the purpose of awakening.

I had been studying ACIM with Jackie and Mia for six months at this point, and when this retreat was over I intended to take my newly found mind training tool, and go back to my beloved alpine village of Wanaka. This place was my idea of heaven on earth and I was going to live there happily ever after. Or so I thought!

During a break, one of the participants asked me out of the blue if I was going to the Peace House with David. I replied, "No, I'm here for the retreat, and then I'll be going back down to the South Island." A little while later, someone else asked me the same question, and again I replied, "No." A third person came up to me and asked if I would be going to America with David! I said, "Not that I'm aware, but I'm open to that possibility." When the fourth person asked me, I said, "I may be." When the fifth person asked me, I said, "Yes!"

I told Jackie about the people coming up to me, and together we went to share the news with David. His response was, "Wonderful!" He told us that Kathy, his secretary of five years, had recently left the ministry to get married, and the young couple who'd lived with him for some time had moved to Canada. The Peace House was left with only David and the cats, Angel and Tripod. Since the cats didn't do a lot of secretarial work, David thought it would be wonderful to have me come and stay for three months as a volunteer.

My body had felt cold for about five years, especially my fingers and toes. By the second day of the retreat I found that my whole being was flooded with warmth. It felt like an inner furnace had been turned on. I was a little embarrassed to find myself heading to the bathroom every couple of hours to splash myself with cold water!

Recently I had shared with my family that I wanted to experience a love that couldn't come to an end. Jackie, being a Course student, quietly beamed in recognition of what I was beginning to realize—that I wanted a "holy relationship"—the love that I wanted was God's.

One morning while David was teaching, I thought I saw a wedding ring on his finger. I was a little surprised, but didn't say anything to anyone. During the session a participant asked him if he would ever get married. He replied that he was very open to the Spirit's plan, however that may unfold. The next day I noticed that David was no longer wearing the ring, and I asked Jackie why he would wear a wedding ring for just one day. She gave me a quizzical look and told me that he hadn't been wearing a ring at all.

The Spirit had already told me that David was going to be my life-partner. I interpreted the ring I had seen on his finger to be a vision telling me that we were to be married. Marrying someone who traveled around talking about God was certainly not the direction that I had planned for my life, and I found myself too taken aback by it all to say anything.

For the next few days, every time David spoke about marriage I could have sworn he was speaking directly to me, although I had my eyes closed most of the time, so I couldn't actually see who he was looking at. My whole being responded to this unmistakable presence of love. I recognized that it was coming from the same source that had radiated through my soul when I had fallen to my knees in surrender. Awareness of this presence was all that I wanted. I didn't know what any of it meant, so I simply basked in the warmth.

The Peace House

The following six weeks were like a fast flowing river. I returned to Wanaka, packed up my belongings and garaged my car at a friend's house. I flew to Cincinnati, where David picked me up at the airport. We drove to the Peace House—a quaint, green, "gingerbread house" from the 1860's set in a quiet, inner-city neighborhood. Inside it was simple, clean and welcoming. As we walked into the living room—appropriately called the sanctuary—it felt as if we had entered a chapel. David told me that I could choose any room as my own. There were two bedrooms downstairs. As we walked past the staircase leading up to two more bedrooms, one of which was David's, I heard the Spirit say, "Take your bags up to David's room." I was shocked! My response to this guidance was, *I'm not that kind of girl!* David, of course, didn't hear a word of this internal dialogue. I walked straight past the staircase and checked out the two rooms downstairs!

And thus my Goldilocks experience began. I tried the coziest room downstairs, but I just couldn't sleep; I was awake all night. I blamed it on the furnace which was, after all, very noisy. The second night I also couldn't sleep. I tried the bed in the other downstairs room for a couple of hours, but I couldn't settle in there either. The third night I went to the couch in the sanctuary, assuming that I was so exhausted by this point that surely I would sleep. But I couldn't.

By the fourth day, I was wrecked. Still recovering from head injuries, sleep was very important to me. Three nights without any sleep was a major problem. I told David I didn't know why I couldn't sleep and asked if he would turn off the furnace. David checked the weather and discovered that there was a blizzard on its way. Turning the furnace off was not an option because the pipes would freeze—and, after all, it was the middle of winter. He said that if I wanted to, I could share the huge king-sized mattress on the floor in his room.

Usually I didn't sleep very well with someone else in the bed, so I thought the chances of me being able to sleep with David were very low. But that night I curled up in his bed, and slept soundly. It was as if I had landed in the most peaceful place in the world. My mind was able to rest, still and silent. There was no doubt that this was where I was meant to be.

Chapter Two

Heart of Service

Winter 2004–2005

"Do you want freedom of the body or of the mind? For both you cannot have. Which do you value? Which is your goal? For one you see as means; the other, end." T-22.VI.1

"Be not disturbed at all to think how He can change the role of means and end so easily in what God loves, and would have free forever. But be you rather grateful that you can be the means to serve His end. This is the only service that leads to freedom." T-22.VI.3

"This holy relationship, lovely in its innocence, mighty in strength, and blazing with a light far brighter than the sun that lights the sky you see, is chosen of your Father as a means for His Own plan. Be thankful that it serves yours not at all. Nothing entrusted to it can be misused, and nothing given it but will be used. This holy relationship has the power to heal all pain, regardless of its form." T-22.VI.4

Serving God

Over the coming week as I rested, I watched David closely. He just didn't seem human! After a few days I realized that what I was seeing was someone who had given himself over so fully to being of service to God that he was being used to maximum potential. He was awake at three a.m., typing away with his two index fingers in the quiet hours while the world was asleep.

Hours later I would watch him put on one hat after another, playing all of the roles that it usually takes an entire spiritual community to fulfill.

He counseled in joy for hours on the phone, answered emails, shared inspirational posts on his Yahoo mailing list, and responded to invitations for gatherings. He also worked on websites, opened the mail, fulfilled requests for CDs, banked checks, cleaned and fueled the car, made dinner, took out the trash, fed the cats, cleaned the litter box and cleared the snow from the path.

Soon I found myself being drawn to help. It was impossible not to. David was serving God, and I could feel the purpose behind each action. I could feel that there was no personal motivation behind any of it. As I watched, it all looked so involuntary—the way he suddenly disengaged from emails and moved towards an outing, or stood up from the table and moved back upstairs. I could feel that he was following the Spirit's movement from within. As soon as I began to offer myself to being of service—even in simple ways like tending to the cats and making tea—I felt immense joy in my heart from being of service to God.

The more I supported David by handling practical tasks, the more he was freed up for counseling calls and emails, which inspired me and drew me into a deeper experience of serving God. I felt an overwhelming sense of gratitude. Even though David shone in recognition and sometimes thanked me, the gratitude I was feeling was coming from deep within my own heart. My whole life, I had wanted to know where I was meant to be, and what I was meant to be doing. The prayer of my heart was finally being answered.

Siestas

Every afternoon I began to get tired, and by two p.m. I was ready for a nap. David loved the idea of siestas—especially as he woke with the Spirit at three a.m. each morning to do his emails—and we fell into the routine of meeting in the sanctuary for meditation each afternoon. I had never experienced such deep meditation so easily. At times I felt as if I were falling. One time I called out to Jesus, feeling like it would be the end of something—me, perhaps. In the quiet of my mind I heard Jesus saying, "Keep letting go. I'm here." So I continued to allow the falling, the total letting go of everything. I usually ended up lying down after about an hour, and falling into a restful sleep. Sometimes we relocated back upstairs to lay down, where I curled up in David's arms and sank into a deep place. I had never allowed myself to drool on anyone before. Instead of feeling embarrassed, I was delighted at how completely comfortable I felt. My priorities were changing, and my ideas of being "perfect" were coming undone.

After a couple of weeks I was still sleeping soundly in David's bed, but keeping my clothes in the bedroom downstairs and using the downstairs shower. I started to feel split from living upstairs but having my things downstairs. I felt the strain of not accepting what was becoming obvious—I was being guided in the direction of an intimate relationship with David by an unseen and indefinable attraction. I couldn't define exactly what the relationship was since I didn't have any past relationships that it could be compared to, or any boxes within which it would fit. It was not that of secretary-employer, girlfriend-boyfriend, or student-teacher. It was so much more than anything that words could describe.

Yet part of my mind was in resistance, insisting that it wasn't a relationship. However, one item of clothing at a time, I began taking my things upstairs and putting them in David's wardrobe. I silently insisted on leaving my toothbrush downstairs until the very last—as a kind of subtle, silent, protest against intimacy. I don't believe David was ever aware of that!

I still had not told anybody about the vision of the ring I'd seen on David's finger that day, or the message I'd heard about David being my life partner. Although it occasionally felt like I was keeping a secret, I rationalized to myself that it didn't make any difference because I would still be doing exactly what I was doing anyway.

Healthy Food Thoughts

I went with David to the local grocery store and found myself in the peanut butter aisle. Although I'd loosened up somewhat from my phase of taking considerable time preparing organic, healthy meals, I still definitely preferred "healthy" to "unhealthy" food. We had already been through the fresh produce area and had gone straight past the tiny organic section without stopping. I assumed that David probably didn't believe in either organic food or pesticides as being causative. I was willing to align with this higher awareness and go beyond purchasing food based on these thoughts.

But while David was getting cereal, I went ahead alone to the peanut butter aisle. Before I knew what was happening, I found myself reading the label on the jar, aghast to find a long list of ingredients. There were nine ingredients! In peanut butter! I grabbed a different brand, and it was the same. I began to read the ingredients and although peanuts, salt, and oil were recognizable—and clearly meant to be there—there were a number of ingredients that didn't sound like food at all, as well as high-fructose corn syrup.

I put the peanut butter back on the shelf and moved along to the jelly section. I checked out the label and again ... high-fructose corn syrup! My mind went into overdrive: *Why is there corn in everything? Is this why so many Americans are overweight? What is with all of these cheap filler ingredients? Why don't Americans question such things? New Zealanders wouldn't stand for this!*

I would eventually learn that the fear-based thoughts I had around food—such as fatty foods are bad for the heart and organic food is good for the body—were all, deep down, a fear of death. I would come to realize that these thoughts were not of God and needed to be released. At the time, however, I just felt paralyzed, unable to choose. Then, thank God, David walked down the aisle.

"David," I asked, "Which brand do you usually get? I'm getting hooked on labels and ingredients, and my mind is going crazy!" He smiled softly and reached out to select a jar of jelly and a container of peanut butter, and we moved on. His very presence was a reminder of the truth, and I redirected my trust and the direction of my thinking to the Spirit. I had a long way to go regarding my food beliefs and grocery shopping. Without mind-watching, my thoughts were sending me off into conspiracy theories, whilst reinforcing a proud patriotic stance!

The Spirit and the Bathroom

Since the age of nineteen, I had worn my hair very short, dyed black, and styled with gel. There was never a stray eyebrow or facial hair to be seen, and my underarms and legs were always clean-shaven. At the Peace House, I was acutely aware of when the next eyebrow hair appeared, but I tried to appear casual and relaxed about my image. After all, I was not meant to care about a *self-concept!*

One day, as I was shaving my legs in the shower, I stopped to ask myself *why?* It was winter! No-one would see them, and David certainly did not care about such things. I laughed out loud at the thought of shaving my legs for David! And then I realized that I actually wanted to be at my desk, replying to a counseling email, and instead I was taking time to shave my legs—which was utterly pointless! I put the razor down and got straight on with where my heart was calling me to be. That was when it dawned on me that asking for guidance was about to go much deeper. There was a lot that I was still doing out of habit, based on assumptions that I had made up along the way in life.

In prayer later I could feel the fear of daring to invite the Spirit into every part of my life. I had never even considered inviting the Spirit into this area. I saw the fear thoughts arise: *What if I'm guided to not take care of my body at all? Will it just be neglected?* The thoughts led to a feeling of dread. I realized that I didn't want to share this with David—if I did, I might have to go through with giving over control—and that was scary.

After allowing these thoughts to roll through my mind, my thoughts turned towards David. Although he brushed his teeth often and showered every day, I knew in my heart that he didn't actually care about the body, and I was surprised to find that I was angry at him for this. I wanted him to care about it! I could feel that I was projecting my fear onto him, and the attack thoughts in my mind started to justify my stance of being separate from him. The longer I allowed the thoughts the worse I felt, so I shared my realizations with David. I felt a depth coming back into my awareness again, a falling back into the deep love that was the purpose of our relationship in God.

Over the following month, I watched my mind and practiced listening to the Spirit. I asked before automatically going through the motions of daily body care. I was relieved to find that I was guided to brush my teeth as usual and to shower every day. The difference was that I was in a loving, listening state of awareness when I did so. My first priority was being with God in prayer. I was often guided to answer emails first and leave the showering and body care until later in the day, rather than doing them in a disconnected, automatic, get-it-done state of mind.

Upon reflection, I recognized that whenever I listened to the ego, I experienced a subtle feeling of sacrifice. But I was learning that the only thing being sacrificed was my peace of mind! Inviting the Spirit in was the total opposite of sacrifice!

Recycling with the Spirit or the Ego?

One day I was feeling stressed; I was beginning to feel resentful about how much cleaning and other work I had to do. After doing the breakfast dishes, I started to wash the cat food tins. David walked into the kitchen right at that moment. He said there was no need to wash the tins, they could go straight into the trash.

As an avid recycler and saver of the planet for more than twenty years, I balked at the idea of not recycling the tins. I started to protest that it was okay, that I could do it. David went immediately to the heart of the matter. Before I knew it, I was receiving a whole teaching on the unreality of the world. David reminded me that the world was made out of hate as a hiding place where God could enter not. He explained that trying to save what was made out of hate was the ego's purpose.

I was unreceptive, and found myself defending against accepting the lesson. In that moment I couldn't see that David was freeing me from performing tasks that were not for the purpose of awakening, and were therefore just another way to maintain my self-concept of being a good caretaker of the world. Core beliefs that I had held my whole life were rubbing up against the Spirit's flow.

I had to admit that I didn't want to wash out the small, smelly and awkward cat food tins, but I could feel the grip in my mind of what it meant to let this go. I had poured a lot of energy into saving the world! Although I was no longer an activist, the beliefs were certainly still in my mind. I felt quietly righteous—I was a good person who recycled everything and was extremely mindful about resources such as electricity and water.

I felt resentment towards David—both because he didn't care and because I was being asked to not care. However, I continued to align my mind with the teachings that I recognized as being the truth. Wow! It was one thing to read them in the Course, but another thing entirely to transfer them to daily life. My resistance started to fall away, and David immediately reflected my openness by saying that we could certainly recycle the large items since they could easily be put in the recycle bins.

David reminded me, "You are not here to work for an organization; everything is here to support us." I would hear this from David whenever the "doer" came up in my awareness and I was taken over by the ego's push to work for any purpose other than forgiveness and love. David reminded me often that the world was a reflection of our mind and could now serve a glorious purpose.

Chapter Three
Yes, I Will Marry You!

Winter/Spring 2005

"The light that joins you and your brother shines throughout the universe, and because it joins you and him, so it makes you and him one with your Creator. … What teaches you that you cannot separate denies the ego. Let truth decide if you and your brother be different or the same, and teach you which is true." T-22.VI.15

Yes!

The word "marriage" kept coming to my mind. In a typical, worldly sense of the concept of marriage, I didn't know what it would mean to marry David. But in another sense I knew exactly what it would mean. Saying yes to marrying David would be a symbol of a deep, lifelong commitment to God. It would mean saying yes to leaving the past, yes to living wherever the Spirit sent me, yes to accepting that David's Calling was also my own, and yes to not leaving. I thought I'd said yes to God before, but with the thought of this total commitment, I could feel fear rising in me; it felt as if saying yes was a brand-new decision to make. I knew that by joining with one who was clearer than me, the little "I" would not be able to hide. This brought up every thought of sacrifice imaginable. I simply had no box to put the concept of marriage into.

As I sat on the sofa in the Sanctuary of the Peace House I dared to ask myself the question, *Am I to marry David?* I felt the answer immediately—it was a joyful, love-filled Yes! A few minutes later, David walked into the room and sat on the other sofa, facing me. Although he had never directly asked me, I looked up and softly said, "Yes, I will marry you." To which David exclaimed, "That is wonderful!" as he shone with happiness. In that moment, I sensed that this arranged marriage was not only for my awakening, but would be a blessing to many. It felt holy, and I knew that many, many miracles would come from it.

Partnership and Clothes

Because my relationship with David felt so different to anything else I had experienced, it took a while for the idea that David and I were a couple to enter my mind. When it did, though, the projections onto David's image started. First, I noticed his clothes. I was as yet unwilling to admit that beneath my façade of "not really caring," I had definite ideas of what was attractive and what wasn't. David didn't appear to have a style, but it was far worse than that. I had watched a few teaching videos in which he was wearing what appeared to be a large women's apricot-colored tracksuit.

Oh, my God! I thought, *What am I doing?* The ego reared up in my mind, telling me point-blank that this could not be my life. How could I possibly be in a relationship with a man who wore a large women's apricot tracksuit?!!!

Thoughts of my father, Roger, entered my mind. If he called now and asked how I was, I wouldn't know how to answer him. If he asked if I were happy, I would have to lie. The golden glow of the miracle was fading from my awareness; instead, I felt the intensity of a split mind. I was experiencing a lot of healing, but the voice of the ego was persistent: *This is not what I would choose, so what am I doing? Am I being manipulated? If I would lie to my family—those who know me better than anyone else in the world—then this is outright wrong.*

I felt a darkness and tension filling my mind and body and, for the first time, I found myself feeling distant from David. But still, I didn't voice my feelings to him. Instead, I tried to ignore the judgmental thoughts, hoping they would go away, but they didn't. Before long, I noticed that my love for David had completely dropped. I knew I had to tell him that I didn't like his clothes. I felt scared because I didn't know what would happen. It could be that he would send me home.

Finally, I got up the courage to share my thoughts. His immediate response was one of happiness! "You can go through the wardrobe and clear out everything you don't like! All of my clothes have been donated, and

I don't wear a lot of them, so that would be wonderful!" The love came back instantly! The next day I happily cleared out six full bags of donated clothing.

A few days later I was still having judgmental thoughts about David's clothes, and again I shared my thoughts with him. Once more, it felt like I was taking a huge risk. I felt like I was exposing the worst of myself, the very part that I would not want him, or anyone else, to know existed. However, I took the risk and told him that I still didn't like his clothes. I shared that they affected the way I felt about him. His response? "Think of me as a Ken doll. You can dress the Ken doll." He looked delighted at the thought of being taken shopping! Oh, my. I just couldn't believe how wrong I had been about what might happen to our relationship if I was totally honest.

Expressing my thoughts was clearly part of the healing. I learned that hiding my thoughts led me to feeling separate not only from David, but from the gift the Spirit was offering through him. However, when I exposed my private thoughts, the miracle was always waiting for me on the other side. I would experience this many, many times throughout the following years.

First Road Trip

I had been at the Peace House for about six weeks when I joined David on my first road trip. David loved getting in his car and going wherever he was invited to hold Course gatherings and shine his light. A string of invitations were going to take us south from Cincinnati to Florida and back. Our first stop was at the Oasis Institute in Knoxville, Tennessee, where we were warmly greeted by our hosts, Steven and Susan.

At the front of the room were two chairs. I was directed to one of the chairs, and a microphone was put in front of me. I felt shivery and exposed, and as I shuffled around trying to get comfortable, I bumped the microphone a couple of times. When it was my turn to speak, I shared that I felt nervous, and since I was so new to the Course, I didn't think I would have anything of value to say.

The audience showered me in love, calling out with their southern accents, "Oh sweetie, don't be scared of us, we love you!" My fear melted away in an instant. I found myself sharing the transformational experiences that I was going through, which perfectly matched up with the high metaphysical teachings that were pouring through David. I felt like I was being used as a bridge—describing in simple, practical terms exactly what the Course teachings meant.

Afterwards a number of participants gave me love-filled hugs. They expressed their gratitude for my sharing, and I realized my function was simply to be honest and authentic, and to speak directly from my own experience.

The "I Know" Mind

On the drive to Knoxville the car had been making a strange sound. It was much like a honking goose, and I observed that it seemed to be happening every time we reached a speed of about seventy miles an hour. My mind had been going through the possibilities of what the problem could be, when after the day's drive the check-engine light came on. My "I know" mind went immediately into full swing. As we arrived at our destination I got under the hood, saying, "My dad taught me about cars. We need to check the oil." We checked the oil, and I found the problem—the oil was below empty. I saw my thoughts: *This is what happens when a mystic who doesn't care about the world owns a car. David is inattentive. Looking after the vehicle is important.*

The "I know" mind is the part of the mind that thinks it knows something about this world. It speaks first and with confidence about what it knows to be true. Its "facts" are always based on past experience in the world, rather than a present connection with the Spirit. Actually, its purpose for communicating these facts is to maintain itself as an identity apart from God.

Since I didn't feel we should drive the car any further without oil, we left it outside the Institute that night and went home with our hosts after the gathering. Back at the Institute the following morning I was under the hood with enough oil to fill the empty tank. David went inside to talk with our hosts. Diligently, I checked the oil level again, and again saw that it was almost out. I began pouring in oil but after adding a very small amount, I had a strong feeling to check the oil level again. I was shocked to see that the oil was over-full!

Perplexed, I stepped back. When David came outside, he saw the look on my face, and he spoke one sentence, "It's the 'I know' mind!" I still insisted that we stop and have a mechanic check out the car because something was definitely not right. We stopped on the way out of town, and a mechanic put his head under the hood and checked things out. With a big smile, he announced that there was absolutely nothing wrong with the car. I was humbled.

We continued on our road trip, and David told me that the check-engine light signified the need to check the mind. On our travels there were many more "undoings" for me and what I thought I knew. On our way back to the Peace House, the check-engine light turned off for no apparent reason, and we burst into laughter, fully embracing the lesson!

The experience of an open mind—a mind that constantly turns to the Spirit for guidance and direction in all matters—is the goal of all learning. The living experience of an innocent mind that no longer pretends to know anything is pure delight! And in this defenseless mind, God is made welcome.

Vows

We continued down towards Florida, where we had a gathering and a dinner with a group of new ACIM friends. We were sharing our marriage guidance with everyone, and a woman asked, "Will it be a real marriage?" I asked what she meant by a "real marriage." She asked, "Will you have vows?" David and I smiled knowingly at each other—we hadn't received guidance to have vows.

David shared our guidance that a legal marriage was not necessary as this involved the government, whereas the purpose of our relationship was a deep commitment to the Spirit. A legal contract felt completely out of alignment with this deep purpose.

"If I had vows," I said as I looked at David, not knowing what I was going to say next but feeling something beautiful coming, "They would be 'I love you now', and 'I trust you.'" We smiled. The vows felt very deep and perfectly in alignment with the marriage—holy, joyful, and new! What else could there be to say?

Rings

One afternoon, during a restful few days in Florida, David said he felt guided to get a wedding ring. I felt a familiar deep fear arise, the same fear that arose when it was time to let go of the past in some way. It was a fear that didn't make sense logically. It was clearly the ego's fear of being exposed and undone. It felt like the fear of death, which I later learned was actually the fear of love. The ego is "killed" by love in the sense that when the light comes, the darkness disappears—it is literally dissolved in the light. Although I had said yes to being married, wearing rings was a "public" step and one from which the ego couldn't hide. It should have been a moment of celebration, but for the undoing of the ego, it was a moment of terror!

On our way to the pier for a walk by the water, and only minutes after sharing his prompt with me about a ring, David pulled into a shopping center. We went into a store, and David bought a gold wedding band! Dealing with a flurry of fear thoughts, and not knowing what to do or say, I found myself hiding behind a nearby clothing rack. I watched David have a joyful encounter over a wedding ring from a safe distance!

David was very happy with his ring, completely unaffected by my subdued state of mind. As we left the store I heard the Spirit clearly say within my mind, "If you drive past the same store on the way back, go in and buy a ring." I sighed with relief; we were taking so many turns on the way to the pier that there was no way we would possibly drive past the same shopping center on the way back!

We had a lovely afternoon walking along the pier by the harbor, while David thoroughly enjoyed his new ring. Still a little nervous about the whole situation and how my life seemed to be unfolding before my eyes so rapidly, I asked David if he would mind if I took a walk by myself. He was more than happy to sit on a park bench by the water, and I continued on down the pier.

I found myself drawn to sit by a fairly scruffy looking man in his seventies, who told me he was from Bulgaria. I'd been to Bulgaria, and we had a beautiful encounter, which felt like divine intervention. I could feel the call for love from this man deep within me, and I immediately felt a deep connection with David. I felt the purpose of our relationship was being fulfilled in this very moment. I had a flashback to previous relationships where I had felt limited by not being able to fully share my love and my heart. Even though my previous partners had not been overly jealous or protective, there was a subtle feeling that the relationship implied ownership or limits of some kind.

And now here I was with this older man, feeling the presence of love arise within me. I knew that David would not want me to hold back. I shared with this man how loved he was, no matter what had seemed to happen in the past, and he lit up before my eyes. His innocence shone brighter and brighter with every moment that passed. The experience was very pure and felt holy! I was overjoyed to be shown directly what this marriage with David was for! I felt as if I were walking on air as I returned to David to share the whole experience with him. He was absolutely delighted, and we hugged and kissed and floated back to the car.

We began the drive back to our friends' house, trusting that somehow we would find the way. And, lo and behold, we went right by the shopping center where David had bought his ring! "Turn left!" flew out of my mouth, and without hesitating, David immediately turned into the parking lot. I told him about my guidance to get a second ring if we passed the same store, and together we went in to find my ring. The jewelry counter assistant appeared to be expecting us!

Spontaneous Wedding Ceremony

David and I had left our wedding ceremony completely in the Spirit's hands. One afternoon I kept hearing the word "garden." I loved the thought of taking a walk through a botanical garden, and after an Internet search, we discovered one close to where we were staying. We found it easily, and it felt wonderful to have a little time together for a walk. We strolled along the pathways, through various garden areas, along a river and over a bridge. All of a sudden, we found ourselves standing in the middle of a wedding garden! It was as if we had been transported to Spain—we were standing on terracotta paving stones, and the high walls around us were covered in bright purple and dark pink bougainvillea flowering vines.

We looked at each other and grinned! Our wedding ceremony was about to happen! One vow after another came from my lips, followed by a kiss. The ones I remember are, "I love you now. I trust you. I love laughing with you. I love being with you. I love sharing this deep purpose with you. I love traveling with you. I love serving God with you."

David shared this celebratory announcement on the mailing list:

> Greetings of Joy! I am happy to announce that Kirsten and I have joined in the purpose of holy relationship and are wearing wedding rings to symbolize the love we share with each other and with everyone. The guidance to get rings came on February 12th, and in between my ring in the morning and her ring in the late after-noon, Kirsten had a holy encounter which symbolizes the love we

share with everyone. She met a seventy-nine year old Bulgarian man while walking. The man told her she had the eyes of an angel, and Kirsten shared her experiences from her travels in Bulgaria.

The man beamed and said it had been many years since he had kissed a woman, and Kirsten softly turned her face and offered him her cheek. After he kissed her they talked some more, and his heart opened. She received many kisses on that cheek before the holy encounter ended, and she returned to me with a huge smile on her face. Love loving ItSelf is what life is all about. Universal love. Unconditional love. It is truly an honor to demonstrate love by living a life of love. This is what marriage and holy relationships reflect. May our lives be a reflection of Divine Love, and honor the Creator in every thought, word, and action that is expressed.

I bask in the peace of the present moment, and I'm honored that Kirsten and I can live, travel, and demonstrate the love within. Holy union is synonymous with living in the present moment, and we share the simple ideas, "I trust you" and "I love you now" as the purpose for everything in our lives. It is a union of Mind that inspires and blesses all the world. It is an expression of laughter and playfulness, spontaneity and glee that shines from heart to heart. It is wonderful to sink into the divine silence together with everyone. It is a delight to accept invitations from around the world and answer God's Call to shine the light of love. Love is simple, and I am happy that Kirsten has joined me in this partnership of expressing love. This relationship is like all our relationships, for it expresses a single purpose. Everyone is included. Since we have been guided to live and travel together and share our love, the symbol of partnership feels helpful and natural. It is a partnership of freedom that supports and nurtures awakening to the Spirit within.

I thank you, Spirit, for the symbol of partnership which reflects holy union. I give thanks to all our sisters and brothers who welcome You into their hearts. I welcome all invitations to join together in your holy purpose and rejoice together as one!

Chapter Four

Volcanos and Honeymoons

Spring 2005

"Before a holy relationship there is no sin. The form of error is no longer seen, and reason, joined with love, looks quietly on all confusion, observing merely, 'This was a mistake.' And then the same Atonement you accepted in your relationship corrects the error, and lays a part of Heaven in its place." T-22.VI.5

Simple, Profound Guidance

Two young Course teachers on their way from Wisconsin to Florida spent the night with us at the Peace House. As they were leaving, one of them looked directly into my eyes and said, "Kirsten, if I could give you one piece of advice for the spiritual journey, it would be: Don't make a decision when you're not feeling at peace."

That wisdom was directly from the Holy Spirit. No doubt about it. This simple and profound guidance became a solid reference point for my mind in times of doubt. In the months and years to come, every time that I wanted to leave, every time that I doubted, it was easy to recognize that I was not at peace. This reference point served as a prompt for me to pause and not act upon or seriously entertain attack thoughts. Rather than drawing conclusions about the cause of my upsets, I inquired within to see the egoic thoughts and beliefs in my mind that were in need of healing. As I practiced with this process, I came to see that following my "doubt thoughts" and drawing conclusions always took me further away from peace and from David.

Each time I went through the process of shifting from anger or fear to a state of reasonable peace, I asked for guidance. The guidance was never what I had thought it would be. I found that there was nothing to do and no action to take based on my fearful thoughts. These reference points were the stabilizing foundation for my mind. They supported me in being able to see that everything was occurring literally for my awakening.

My other reference point was to trust David. When I first heard this guidance it felt very significant. However, I was afraid because I believed I was being asked to put my full faith and trust in a man. I went into prayer and asked what Jesus meant when he told me to "trust David." He said, "Trust me through him. Trust David's devotion. Trust that the only purpose he has is Awakening, and therefore he is turning to me constantly for everything. David is one who has been given to you as a symbol of being able to trust me."

It felt like a leap of faith to trust David—a leap that I would make many, many more times. I didn't realize it at first, but it felt like a leap because I was going through a process of withdrawing my faith from the ego's familiar thought system and placing it in the Spirit, in the unknown.

Divorce with the Spirit

A friend of David's from Argentina invited him to visit in late March to hold a series of gatherings. David immediately included me in the plans. We went ahead and bought our plane tickets. They were the cheapest tickets available and were non-refundable and non-changeable. Two days before we were due to leave, our host Maria wrote to David saying that she needed to cancel our trip and the planned ACIM gatherings because a family situation had arisen.

David called her immediately. She sounded terrible; her voice had dropped two octaves. She poured out her heart—her beloved husband of forty years had told her he was leaving her as he was in love with another woman. And to make matters worse, the other woman was their maid, who was a dearly beloved member of their extended family.

David knew without a doubt that this trip was guided by the Holy Spirit, and canceling it was not possible for him. His voice was gentle and certain as he told her that we couldn't cancel the trip because of our non-refundable tickets. "Besides!" he said happily, "Kirsten and I are coming on a honeymoon!" Somehow, this was the perfect thing to say, and Maria's voice lifted back up to its normal pitch: "A honeymoon? Oh, that's wonderful!" My eyes grew large watching how the Spirit had answered Maria's call for love through David, with a perfect redirection for her mind.

Our flight was overnight with two stops, and although Argentina was south of Cincinnati, our first flight took us north. As we descended into Chicago around 11:30 p.m., I found myself saying, "David, I see us staying in a comfortable hotel tonight!" David smiled, "Well, our flight is scheduled to continue to Buenos Aires tonight, but we'll see." As we walked through the airport, there was an announcement: "US Airways Flight 323 has been delayed due to technical difficulties. Please proceed to customer service for further information." David and I grinned at each other and happily walked to the service desk to stand in line with a hundred or so others.

Some of the people in the line were complaining about the flight delay, but David and I were happy. We knew that everything was working together, not just for our good, but for our utmost joy! And the joy spread—I couldn't help but share with people that we were on a mission from God and that the Spirit was taking care of everything. I told them about my feeling that we would stay in a hotel instead of spending the night on a plane, and how miraculous it was that this was all being arranged for us. Our experiences were all lessons in non-judgment.

By the time we got to the counter, the staff were in the flow of handing out meal and hotel vouchers. We happily caught the free shuttle to a lovely hotel, took warms baths, and snuggled up in fluffy bathrobes. To top it off, we gleefully ordered room service with our meal vouchers—apple pie with vanilla ice cream!

What abundance! How loved we are! We had a wonderful night's sleep and caught our flight the next morning, arriving fresh for our two weeks of gatherings and miracle working. I was deeply grateful to be shown how taken care of we are by God. Like softly spoken poetry in my mind, I remembered some of Jesus' quotes from the Bible and the Course: "Put the Kingdom of Heaven first and all things shall be added unto you." (Matthew 6:33) "When you have learned how to decide with God, all decisions become as easy and as right as breathing. There is no effort, and you will be led as gently as if you were being carried down a quiet path in summer." T-14.IV.6 "Do you really believe you can plan for your safety and joy better than He can? You need merely cast your cares upon Him because He careth for you. You are His care because He loves you." T-5.VII.1

Maria and her soon-to-be-ex-husband came to pick us up together. Regardless of whether he loved another woman or not, she loved him deeply and was absolutely set on having the spirit of forgiveness lead the way through every step that they were to take together.

I had never experienced this before, and I was struck by her maturity and devotion to a true holy relationship. She was looking deeply at the belief in abandonment and betrayal, while "staying the Course" and refusing to turn away from love. Maria was a living demonstration of forgiveness as she openly explored the dissolution of her marriage and family situation in an atmosphere of prayer. Again, I felt the depth of where the Course was leading.

We spent the week with Maria and her family, and then David and I headed south to hold several gatherings in rural areas before heading further south to our "honeymoon" destination.

I Feel Like a Handbag

An uncomfortable feeling had started to arise within me during the last few gatherings with David. All of the teaching was pouring through him, while I hardly spoke. I sat on a chair beside him, sometimes closing my eyes or gazing around looking at the audience. Sometimes I didn't know where to look!

When a participant asked a question, I would often hear something that I felt would be very helpful to say, but in my perception, David always answered so quickly that I didn't have a chance to speak. And then when he would turn to me, he would often give such a long introduction to my experience that I didn't know what to say when he asked me to talk further about it!

After the second gathering in the rural areas of Argentina, my annoyance was rising: *I feel like an accessory to the Mystic. David is the Mystic. Everyone wants to hear him speak, and I'm just sitting on this chair like a handbag.*

As usual, I had no choice but to share the egoic thoughts with David. There was no way I could "pretend" and put on some kind of show for the next gathering. His sincere response was, "Oh, you can start the next gathering off then." I immediately felt fearful and knew that wasn't really the answer I had wanted to hear. I didn't feel confident enough to start the gathering myself. I was well aware that David's Presence somehow brought everyone into a shared experience of depth. Sharing the thoughts felt good, and although there wasn't a solution in form, something within me relaxed.

During the next gathering, I felt very content sitting beside David. I had dropped back into the experience that it was all for me, and I loved listening to every word that came out of his mouth. At one point I spoke, and at the end of the gathering a beautiful, devoted spiritual teacher looked at us both and said softly, "She has the same gift as you do, David." Beaming, David replied, "Oh yes, she does." I have no idea what I said during that gathering, but I did know that my sense of competition and pride had disappeared.

The Honeymoon and the Volcano

After the gatherings we traveled south to Miramar on the coast. David was delighted as we arrived at the lovely Oasis of Peace hotel for our four-day honeymoon by the ocean.

I, on the other hand, was not filled with delight. I was suffering from holding on to private thoughts, and the longer I held back from speaking them to David, the wider the gulf between us was becoming. Every time David mentioned the word "honeymoon," I felt the hit of the private thoughts that were building up within my mind. When we were with other people, or holding gatherings, I was drawn into being of service to the Spirit, and the ego thoughts faded completely out of awareness. However, when we were alone, they would come right back into my awareness—blocking love completely.

After two days, I felt quite separate from David as I still hadn't shared my attack thoughts. I kept trying to forgive them and hand them over to the Spirit, but nothing was changing. On the third night, we went around the corner to a little French restaurant where we were the only customers.

David continued to shine and glow as if there was no problem at all, but it had reached an unbearable point for me. I couldn't continue another moment. And so I spoke all of the thoughts that were in my mind—horrible, judgmental, and embarrassing thoughts about teeth, breath, bodily noises, bathroom towels, clothes, and fashion. David wore knee-high white socks with sandals, which was not cool where I came from! I knew I couldn't hold anything back, so I let it all out. I told him that I didn't feel like this was a honeymoon, it didn't feel at all romantic, and I felt like I was a liar and a fake every time he mentioned the word. I told him that I felt like I couldn't say anything because I didn't really know what any of it was for. What was the point in saying any of it since I should just be able to change my mind about my thoughts? I expressed how the thoughts came up every day, and I just couldn't handle it anymore.

Intuitively, the staff kept a safe distance as I spoke to David. It seemed so personal and horrible, but I felt that I truly had nothing to lose. After all, I was almost at the end of my three-month stay in the U.S., so I was due to return to New Zealand soon anyway.

I was sure this was the end. David would agree that I had done my best and the relationship would be over. Instead, he reached across the table and took my hands. He looked deeply into my eyes and said, "Now we can begin the relationship." I couldn't believe it. Tears fell down my cheeks as a wave of innocence flooded through me.

Once again, it was the total opposite of what I feared would happen. Our relationship depended on me daring to be transparent, daring to share the thoughts when they arose, daring to face the fear of rejection and punishment of some kind. When I withdrew from David in my mind, I was effectively ending the relationship anyway. Once again, I saw that I didn't really have a choice. I either said "yes" to this holy relationship and the Spirit's purpose, or I pulled away and cut myself off from my connection with the Spirit and David. In knowing this, I felt more confident about just going for it!

The waitress then brought our menus, approaching our table with a big smile and loving eyes. David and I had a wonderful evening, and the rest of our time in Argentina was a joyful, loving, soft experience. Everyone we met reflected the depth of love I had fallen back into. We laughed as everyone we saw—from teenagers outside the music store, to policemen on duty, to dogs on the streets—greeted each other with multiple kisses on the cheeks!

As we flew back to the U.S., we were deeply grateful for all of the healing that had occurred on our trip. I was glowing with love and happiness as I approached the immigration officer to show him my passport. I told him that I only had a few days left with my visa-waiver status, and although I was due to return to New Zealand soon, I would love to stay longer if it was possible. He told me that I couldn't extend a visa-waiver, and he asked me what I was doing in the U.S., I explained that I was recovering from a head injury and had devoted my life to God and forgiveness. I said that I was part of a ministry and was accompanying my friend on some of his travels, and how wonderful it all was. The immigration officer began to glow as he said, "Well, I can't extend your visa-waiver, but I can give you a new one!"

No wonder we were meant to go to Argentina! Once again, I was amazed at how the Spirit was orchestrating everything without my effort. With the biggest smile, I skipped through to the baggage carousel to meet David!

The Purring Ones

It was a wonderful feeling arriving back at the Peace House knowing that I could stay in the U.S. for another three months. I loved the fact that I was not personally in charge of making anything happen. The Spirit was in control of the plan of my life, and He was making everything clear and obvious—including staying in the U.S. and continuing to be with David. I was being shown the way, step by step.

Tripod, a little three-legged tortoiseshell cat, and her sister Angel, were living with us. They were stray kittens that had been found nearby. Angel loved being outdoors all year round. As long as David played doorman, she would happily go in and out of the front door repeatedly. We laughed at how sincere she was about wanting to be exactly where she was not!

Tripod was highly sensitive and easily frightened, but she responded quickly to love. She lived mostly in David's room, basking in the glow of their holy relationship—meditating on his bed, hopping to his desk, and rubbing at his chair legs until he dropped his hand to her, to receive her love and affection. She had embraced me immediately, initiating "love-fests" whenever I was near her. She had so much love to extend, she could hardly contain herself—she often woke me up, nuzzling into my hair and purring.

When we watched movies the cats would reflect the theme of the film. During a relationship movie they curled up on the back of the sofas, purring contentedly. Whilst watching *The Matrix*, we were stunned by the acrobatic show they put on! Racing around the sanctuary, taking turns chasing each other, and flying in and out of sight around the furniture. At one point they were bounding up to each other. Angel reached out a paw, batting Tripod across the cheek just as Neo and Morpheus had been doing in their training program in the movie. Tripod attempted to bat Angel back. Only having three legs, her little "nub" just wiggled around, giving Angel the advantage!

We watched in total joy as they took off again, disappearing behind the sofas. By now we had paused the movie since the girls had our full attention. Angel crept to the center of the sanctuary in slow motion. Tripod, seeing her chance, hopped out from behind a chair and headed towards Angel as fast as she could. Angel leapt straight up in the air with her legs and paws outstretched—she had turned into Trinity from *The Matrix*! We gasped in amazement as Tripod, in total confusion, looked around for her highly skilled sister, not knowing where she had gone! Angel landed beside Tripod, batted her a couple of times, and they both took off, leaving us to watch the rest of the movie in glee.

Fitness and the Body

As I deepened in my relationship with the Spirit, I was loosening from the belief that my body was my identity or my home. I listened to a talk of David's called "Concern for the Body," where he said that by being concerned about it, I was reinforcing my belief in separation. Since my head injuries, I hadn't been to a gym or gone running at all. I often took walks, and when there was a pool or a beach nearby, I went swimming. Although I was no longer walking or swimming to consciously improve or maintain a level of physical fitness, I had to admit that the beliefs about those things were still there in my mind.

I had already given over control of my personal hygiene routines to Spirit, and I felt the same fear in the pit of my stomach at the thought of giving over my attention to physical fitness. The thought of being trapped in an overweight, lethargic body was horrifying to me. I watched the fearful thoughts turn to blame and began projecting them onto David: *Do I have to look at these beliefs now? I'm not David, so why do I have to do what he does? I like to take walks; they're good for me. I'll die if I can never take another walk.* I felt like I was being controlled and told what to do; I was afraid of not being allowed to decide for myself.

I sat with these thoughts, allowing the fear, and invited the Spirit into my mind: *I want to see. Help me to see what is beneath this.* When I prayed and felt into the truth of the experience, I realized that there was still a push, a "drive" at times with my walks.

Sometimes the walks were gentle and spacious, but I had to admit that at other times they were not gentle; their purpose was not loving. I could see how I had been lying to myself by pretending that what I was doing was caring for myself, when the ego's reinforcement of body identification was right there, clear as day. It was no longer disguised, and I could no longer lie to myself. Beyond all else I wanted the Peace of God—to know my true identity as Spirit.

A sneaky, justifying thought flashed across my mind: *I'll give this over to the Spirit, but I can always take a walk for the purpose of forgiveness.* Damn it! I still wanted to be able to keep going for walks under the pretense of a spiritual purpose. I still felt the split; I didn't fully trust that I could let it go. I was still afraid. Finally, I took a deep breath and gave it all over to the Spirit in prayer.

I felt that letting go of my identification with the body might take a while. However, I'd noticed that the more I dived into the Spirit's purpose and was around David—who was such a clear demonstration of one purpose—the more the areas of my life that were laced with the ego's motivation were brought to my attention. My mind felt like a sieve that was being gently shaken—all that was soft and fine could fall through, but any little rocks were brought into view so that they could be removed.

One day I was particularly stressed with ego resistance and was about to go for a walk, but David told me that I was to stay and talk it through with him. He told me there was nothing magical or causative about walking, and I could do the healing right there sitting in the very place that I felt so desperate to leave. It was intense. But I was willing, and after exposing the fears, the desire to walk dissolved away in peace.

Identification with the body and the desire to be fit was to be an ongoing mind training practice for years to come. I'm happy to say that walking and swimming continued to be used as ways of joining with "mighty companions," and I had many mystical experiences in nature. Just as with personal hygiene, this area of my mind was absorbed into the totality of a prayerful life. And despite the ego's fears, the lesson was that there was "no sacrifice." The only thing that was given up was the pain.

I Want to Be Eaten by a Bear

After a couple of weeks at the Peace House, David and I were in our car, headed north on a road-trip to Vermont. Until this day, David had happily joined me for what I still felt were my essential afternoon "siestas." Usually we managed to work siesta time into our travel schedule wherever we went, either by stopping in rest areas or arriving at our destination in time for a nap. However, on this day, we were at least three hours from our destination, and it was nearing two p.m.

I noticed the typical thoughts that arose within my mind when I began to feel the familiar heaviness, and it seemed like my rest time was threatened: *If we don't stop soon I will start to get a headache. I'm starting to fade and I need to have a rest. I won't make it for the gathering tonight.* I asked David to pull the car over. I could sense that he wasn't in full agreement, but I was clear and firm in my request—after all, I was still recovering from a head injury, and he knew it was what I needed.

After not seeing a rest area for some time, David pulled the car over on the side of the road, and we attempted to rest. We reclined the front seats and lay on our sides. David's large six-foot frame hardly fit into the tiny hybrid car, and he shuffled around, unable to stretch his legs out at all. Vehicles flew by, shaking the car, and it was anything but restful. The awareness that this was not the Spirit's Plan was like a deafening unspoken sound that filled the vehicle.

After ten minutes, David sat up, adjusting his seat, and said we would continue driving. He said it wasn't restful, that he had a gathering that night, and that our hosts were expecting us at 5:30 p.m. for dinner. We were to continue, and I could rest in the car as he drove. I protested that the car was too low to the ground, that I felt jarred by the pot-holes. I was worried about being exhausted by the time we got there. However, David was clearly following the Spirit's guidance, and I had no choice. I felt terrible. Trapped. I wondered what I was doing there anyway in a crazy little car that David had bought simply to save gas. I was in total disagreement with him about everything in that moment. Then the dark thoughts turned to hurt—David obviously didn't love me. If my mother, Jackie, was here, she'd find us a hotel to rest in if that was what I needed.

I kept my eyes closed for the rest of the drive. My mind still felt stuck in a dark cloud when we arrived at our hosts' retreat center. David was ready to join with them, but I told him I was going to rest. I lay down in the bedroom, but I felt anything but restful. So instead, I slipped out the back door and went for a walk. As I walked through the pine forest, I thought, *I hope I get eaten by a bear—then David would feel sorry for not loving me!* I walked for another five minutes and then suddenly stopped. *Oh, my God, what was I doing? Wanting to be eaten by a bear? Convinced that David didn't love me? This is ridiculous!*

I had to question the belief that David didn't love me. What if he had been right, that we were supposed to keep driving? I saw the protesting thought arise immediately: *I'm still recovering from a head injury, and he is supposed to be supporting me.* But then I asked myself, *Is that what I really want—to still be recovering from a head injury and be dependent on afternoon naps?* The answer was immediate: *No! I don't want this anymore!*

I didn't know how recovery could be possible. I had tried everything I could to heal myself of my post-accident symptoms—from physical therapies, meditation, pushing my way through them, to surrendering to them. Finally I had accepted that my symptoms might be a lifelong condition; clearly, I had no control over them. It felt like a critical "eye-of-the-needle" moment. I couldn't imagine how healing could occur or how there wouldn't be painful consequences if I missed my afternoon siestas.

But what if this was the day? What if the Spirit really was in charge and this wasn't what it seemed? I had a decision to make: to continue to try to protect myself and be right about what I thought I needed, or to decide for God and to put myself and all of my situations into His hands. My decision was clear—I *did* want to be over this! I *did* want to be healed!

I turned back towards the retreat center and felt a lightness and joy re-entering my mind. I could still feel a faint, familiar sensation of afternoon heaviness in the background, but I happily decided to no longer let that feeling be a reason to make decisions. *From now on,* I told the Spirit, *I give my rest time to you. I trust that if I am to rest, you will guide me.*

Oh, how simple! I found myself skipping back to share the good news with David and everyone at the center. I opened the door and they were all sitting at a large dinner table in a soft, loving glow, as if awaiting my perfectly timed arrival.

The soft glow remained throughout the entire weekend. I felt a quiet strength growing within me, and I felt held in the arms of God. I felt more deeply joined than ever with David in a glorious purpose. These experiences were showing me that I didn't know my own best interests. The Spirit was guiding me through this awakening process step by step for this learning. I was so grateful for David's "true empathy" and non-compromising approach to following the Spirit's guidance.

Chapter Five

Diving Deeper

Spring/Summer 2005

"All that is asked of you is to make room for truth. You are not asked to make or do what lies beyond your understanding. All you are asked to do is let it in." T-21.II.7

Recognition of the Spirit

David and I continued our journey north to Ottawa, Canada to visit his friend, Maureen, and hold several gatherings. Arriving at her house, Maureen opened the door to greet us. When our eyes met, I felt an immediate recognition and familiarity. It felt like meeting a sister, and I was absolutely delighted! Her eyes lit up, and she exclaimed, "Oh! You're a female David!" Later she told me that it was as if a small, female version of David had come to her front door. She knew immediately that she could trust me and that she would be baring her soul to me. She had hesitated to share some things with David because he was a man, but feeling the same Presence in my female form felt very safe and comforting to her.

This kind of encounter—where I was recognized as a miracle worker and immediately trusted—felt like a beautiful confirmation of the truth of who I was. Although David always shared my learning and healing experiences with respect, I was mostly aware of my egoic thoughts and patterns. Meeting Maureen strengthened my sense of worthiness and made me feel even closer to David. Later I read in the Manual for Teachers: "How many teachers of God are needed to save the world?" M-12 The teachers of God are one. This body is the medium through which God's Voice can communicate with those who do not realize they are Spirit. This body they can see, this voice they understand without fear; therefore, the truth is welcomed through this form.

A Very Dark Moment

During our three-day drive back to the Peace House I noticed feelings of pride, and an annoyance with David arising. I wanted to take a leisurely drive, walks in nature, and generally do things differently to David. Arriving back at the Peace House, we unpacked the car, and David went straight into his function of answering emails. As I sat in the sanctuary I felt a darkness arising in my mind—I felt trapped. Over the previous months, many of the ego's "Plan B's" for a different life had been exposed and shared with David, and I knew that there was no going back. I wanted to be free, but when the familiar *I want to be elsewhere* thoughts arose, I felt a grating hatred that I had no choice. I felt controlled and held against my will. Taking walks was no longer an avenue of escape, and a dark, empty, feeling of horror was rising from somewhere deep within the recesses of my mind.

Right on cue, David came downstairs and began talking to me incessantly. Unable to hear him and wanting to get away, I said I was going for a walk. He continued to look straight at me, talking. I felt trapped. I insisted I was going for a walk and he simply continued talking! I walked out and put my shoes on. He followed me out the door, still talking. I couldn't really hear what he was saying as we walked down the street. I thought he was crazy and that anyone who saw us would think so too. He was talking on and on to me about purpose, and commitment and guidance—it wasn't making sense. The voice in my own mind was much louder. My anger at this crazy guy and this crazy life blocked out everything he was saying. Arriving back at the Peace House, he continued following me.

Contained now within the safety of the sanctuary, dark feelings arose within me. I looked at David and was terrified when I thought I saw little horns coming up from his forehead! *Oh, my God!* He continued talking, as if holding me still by his very presence. I had no idea what he was saying, but somehow I was able to stay in the room. Fear rose and consumed me, but within seconds it broke. When I looked again at David, he was pure innocence. His beautiful blue eyes were holding me with the love and kindness of Christ. I could breathe, and realized for a second that I knew all of this was a deep experience of healing *within my mind*. Nothing was what it seemed. The darkness rose again. Once more my perception of David shifted from love to fear; David stayed with me until the horrible feeling vanished. His talking slowed, and his voice quieted until again I could see he was the presence of love. Then it was over.

I wondered how David had known to come downstairs at that very moment, how he'd known what to do and how to help me. I couldn't believe how deeply held and loved I was by a presence and awareness that was far beyond what I could understand. My faith was again restored, and my trust deepened beyond measure. I saw everything so clearly after that experience. I realized that the ego's tricks of wanting personal freedom and having escape plans were all a way of keeping me stuck. It was the exact opposite of the truth! I had fallen into true freedom: being held in God's Love, free from the gnawing discontent of the ego. Oh, what amazing grace! What gratitude I had for David's devotion!

Nothing Fits!

I began to feel that my clothes didn't suit me anymore. I didn't know what to wear because I'd bought my clothes based on judgments about the image I'd wanted to portray at the time. I didn't feel like that same person now, and I felt guilty wearing clothes that reminded me of my old motivations. Now I wanted to be "spiritual" and not care—but secretly, I did!

David always talked about everything being provided by the Holy Spirit, including clothes. However, I still wanted some control over what I looked like, even though I felt impotent about the situation. I had felt the strain of caring but not wanting to care for some time. I'd tried to go shopping and buy clothes a couple of times. Since I didn't know what to buy because my mind was unclear, it simply hadn't worked. Nothing seemed to fit. I finally admitted to the Spirit that I didn't know my own best interests in this department and gave the area over to Him to guide. Over the following months, I watched as my wardrobe was slowly replaced by clothes that were given to me. Everything that was offered fit perfectly, and because it was given freely to me with love, I had no judgment about it at all! Each time I was offered a gift of clothing I was filled with love and gratitude.

I was beginning to experience Divine Providence. It was so gentle and loving to simply receive what the Spirit wanted to give me, rather than try to get something for myself.

One afternoon, I had the thought of needing a thin fleece since the ones I had were too heavy to wear inside. An hour later, our friend Pam called to say that she had a couple of thin fleece sweaters she thought I might like! We were both delighted to experience Divine Providence together. She was just as thrilled as I was to see how she was being used by the Spirit through listening to guidance. Over the next two years, Pam found herself out shopping several times, buying items of clothing that were exactly what I needed, right down to a bikini top to match some bottoms I had. We were amazed every time at how taken care of we are by the Spirit.

Sam the Cat

A question had been arising in my mind about *how to be*. I sat and pondered, *If everything is an illusion, including the people, then what does it mean to be loving towards another person? What would David do if a child or an animal needed help in the moment?* I could feel the fear in my stomach of not knowing. *Would he just stand by and do nothing since it's all an illusion?* I prayed that I would be shown the answer.

The following day as we pulled into our driveway after running errands, Sam, the big white cat from next door, was there to greet us, meowing loudly. He was super-affectionate as we got out of the car, giving us very loving looks all the way down the front path. The following day the exact same thing happened.

Tripod liked to sit at the front door gazing from the window panes that came right down to her level. She perched on her back legs like a squirrel, her front paw resting on the window sill, as she watched the birds and enjoyed the sun. Suddenly, Sam appeared at the window pane right in front of her! She began to whimper, and then whine. The sound increased in volume until it resembled an air-raid siren! Sam continued to be super-friendly to us for the next few days, and upset Tripod numerous times by coming up "her" front steps and looking in "her" door.

After seeing boxes on the verandah at Sam's house, I asked his owner if they were moving. He said that they were and that they were all ready to go except that they didn't know what to do with Sam. "Oh, he's taken care of that. He's been telling us all week that he's moving in with us," I said with a laugh.

On the day that the neighbors moved out, Sam was ready and eager to come inside the Peace House. He skipped in, weaving around David's legs. Tripod, her fur standing on end, went off like a siren again; this time, the sound was interspersed with growls. She looked traumatized. Her eyes were huge, and no matter how loudly she wailed, this huge intruder was not leaving "her" house. Tripod's sister Angel came running into the kitchen and joined in, wailing and hissing at Sam.

Sam froze with his front paw in mid air, a bewildered look on his face. After all, he was simply following his guidance! David scooped Sam up, and he was instantly off Tripod's "intruder alert" radar. The kitty-siren stopped immediately and everyone relaxed. A few minutes later David put Sam down on the kitchen floor, and the siren started again. David moved swiftly and with no apparent emotional concern; he didn't show any false empathy for the animals, and he wasn't trying to control or protect them. He scooped Sam up and set him down a few more times, and then gently placed him on a kitchen chair. Soon, Tripod dashed out of the kitchen and back upstairs to David's room.

Sam had learned that it was much quieter when he was up high, and so he moved about on top of furniture throughout the following month while Tripod's reactions to his presence gradually softened. Here was the answer to my question. The intervention had been handled with certainty and kindness. David had acted in a way that was truly most helpful for all.

Sharing My Journals Worldwide

During various travels with David people had expressed to me, "It must be so much easier for you than it is for us, Kirsten, because you are with David." I knew that in one way it was, and on the other hand they didn't have a clue how intense it was and what I was going through just by being in his presence! Imagine being with a very clear mirror, and you have asked for all of your unconscious darkness to come up to be seen and released. With the nature of projection being what it is, many of the dark thoughts and annoyances were projected directly onto David.

I was new to exposing private thoughts and still wanted to be a "nice" person. Now I had the added pressure of wanting to be a good "spiritual" person, a successful Course student, and teacher of God. Admitting the ego thoughts in my mind continued to make me feel like a failure.

I began to feel inspired at the thought of sharing my journal-writing with the world. I had received such incredible support in practicing forgiveness through this process that I knew it wasn't for me alone.

Every morning upon waking I would move to the couch in readiness for my date with the Spirit. Whenever I had questions, I prayed to the Spirit, something I had been doing since I began studying the Course. Sometimes I found myself speaking directly to Jesus, particularly in times of great intensity. He tended to use few words and give very direct instructions and reminders of the truth.

With my Course book and journal at hand, I turned inward in prayer to connect with the love of my life. It was the most precious thing in the world.

I willingly opened my mind, desiring to share everything, to hide nothing, and to receive all that the Spirit and Jesus wanted to me to know. I began by saying, *Good morning, Holy Spirit* within my mind, and then I would wait and listen, with pen in hand, ready to write down whatever came. I would feel moved to turn to a particular page in the Course, or a question would arise in my mind.

Often, unresolved thoughts from the previous day would come, and I would begin by writing them down. It felt so safe, sitting in the quiet of the early morning, sharing my heart in this way. And then the Spirit's response would begin flowing out through my pen onto the paper. Time and time again I was shown that the attack thoughts that I was afraid to speak aloud were actually the gateway to forgiveness, deeper understanding, and love.

I was receiving profound answers from the Spirit that were from beyond my own realm of understanding. Occasionally I would scribble out what I had just written, thinking that it made no sense at all. However, a few days later I would come back and read what I had scribbled out—and find myself in tears at how deep, clear, and loving the message was. The channeling was a direct experience of God's love moving through me. It was a daily witness to the fact that God was real, and that my faith in the "unknown" was justified.

David often posted beautiful messages on his global mailing list, and he invited me to share my writings on it, too. I felt a bit frightened at first; I was afraid of being judged and of being seen as unhealed. Beyond these thoughts, though, I could feel the inspiration of the Spirit's guidance to be completely transparent and share the depth of my experiences in a direct way. I realized that the fear was the ego's fear of being exposed and undone, which was all the more reason to go for it!

Chapter Six

My Life Is Not My Own

Summer 2005

Listen to the feeling
that calls you into silence,
feel my love surrounding you
and know that you are Home.
I am always with you
and as the memory of your holiness
returns to your awareness
you will remember me.
Wake up my precious child,
so long you have been
in such deep slumber,
dreaming that we were apart
and that you couldn't find
your way Home.

Personal Responsibility

I knew my calling was mysticism—to leave the world entirely and be free of all ownership, responsibility, and ties. Even though Jackie had introduced me to *A Course in Miracles*, I felt guilty because I knew my family wouldn't want me to leave them behind. They would love for me to return from my overseas travels, settle down nearby, and start a family. It was fine to have a spiritual practice and to devote some time to this, but devoting my entire life was not something that any of us had expected. Each step I took to let go of the past was a step out of the world. I was consciously releasing myself from everything, clearing the way so that my direction would be into the unknown, towards God rather than staying with the familiarity of the past.

My father Roger seemed to speak my doubt thoughts aloud and amplify them for me in such a way that I couldn't avoid facing them. For example, he wanted to keep my car, my bike, and some bedroom furniture at the family house so that I would come back and use them. He questioned every step I took that wasn't in the direction of being physically close to him. And while I was still going through a development of trust with the Spirit, I felt challenged by the way he spoke to me as my father—a protective role he'd said many times would always be his.

Journaling

Kirsten: Good morning, Holy Spirit. I need help! I feel stressed because I will be leaving to visit my family in New Zealand soon. I want to know how long to visit them, whether I will be going away on trips to hold gatherings, and what to do with my belongings there.

"The peace of God is my one goal." W-205 I want to remember that I need add nothing to His plan. Right now I feel pain and angst as I feel personally responsible for making decisions and plans, and I believe that in the end, no matter what I do my family will be disappointed. I am trying to plan around what I think will make them happy, and then I feel resentful towards them at how difficult I believe they are making it for me. I can't win! I also feel the sadness that is underneath my stress; they don't want to lose me, and I don't want to lose them.

I'm afraid to let go of familiar parts of my life, such as my car, my rental house, my bed, and my skis. They were reasons to keep coming back to New Zealand, and now it is clear that my life is going in a whole new direction. I feel attached to the belongings, and part of me doesn't want to let them go.

Holy Spirit: You are innocent. You can do no wrong. Every moment of your life is devoted to purpose. I am with you every step of the way. You can trust this.

Kirsten: I offer my faith to you, Holy Spirit, so that you will place it in the Holy place where it belongs: in Truth, in God. I know that you would have me relinquish my plans and join with you in God's plan, which is the end of all heartache.

I sank into the realization that I simply couldn't work it out myself. The basis of my planning was avoiding guilt and trying not to hurt others. I had to let it go. I sat in prayer and had a vision of offering a bunch of lilies to everyone that I had involved in my imaginary plans. The tension melted away, and a tear rolled down my cheek as I felt their innocence and my own. I was then able to go ahead with arranging my flight to return to New Zealand later in the month.

The Chat Room and the Mouse

Some friends started an online chat room called "ACIM-Gather," as a place to invite teachers and students in support of their journey with the Course. David and I were invited to hold the Friday night session whenever available. The talks often started with us sharing miracles and adventures from the road, followed by questions from participants about ACIM and our experiences of living it. Deeper questions from the heart would also be asked regarding how to practically apply the Course teachings to personal struggles and situations. This lead to an outpouring of depth and clarity from David, and often in the final minutes there was a deep stillness that was so palpable it felt as if we were all in the same room. It was a wonderful way to stay connected with an extended ACIM family around the world.

One night we held the talk sitting at David's computer at the kitchen table. During the talk, Sam ran into the kitchen to show us a mouse he had just caught. I continued to focus on the call. The mouse escaped from Sam's clutches and scurried for safety up my leg and into the folds of my skirt! I was so present with what I was saying in that moment that I remarked, "Oh! A mouse just ran up my skirt," and continued right on with the teaching.

Sitting beside David, whose presence and focus is so strong and bright, and knowing that I could be asked a question or called upon to speak at any time, had drawn me deeply into the present moment. This state is a heightened awareness of truth that feels expansive, vibrant, and still.

With full attention on inner listening, nothing of the world can disturb or distract attention away from what is to be heard or spoken. The purpose of awakening is so strong that a mouse running up a leg was like a candle flickering slightly in a breeze, and then continuing to shine its light as if nothing had happened.

A few times when we were hosting from the Peace House, the Internet would go out completely at some point during the talk. David would just smile happily, put his headset away, and say, "That's the end!" I loved to see how totally accepting he was—there was nothing to finish or fix. This was a beautiful illustration of "Let all things be exactly as they are." W-268

Letting Go and Letting God

Over the past week, my mind had become filled with thoughts about other possibilities for my life. Before I knew it, I was feeling physical pain as well as mental anguish due to my split desire. As soon as I shared my thoughts with David, love and trust returned. The pain disappeared too, because it had come from holding on to my will and resisting God's Will for me.

Journaling

Kirsten: Good morning, Holy Spirit. I realize I was resisting your Will. I think this is all being stirred up because I am going back to New Zealand soon to apply for a visa to live in the U.S., it's a big commitment. After exposing all of the doubt thoughts and fears with David this morning about fully committing to being here, I said "yes" again. Yes to our marriage, to God, to the end of hypotheticals, to the end of loss, and to the end of longing for the past. I heard the ego cry out, "Nooooo, you've been tricked! This is not your will!" But it didn't stand a chance.

This morning I was guided to read about sickness being a decision, an attempt to replace God. I don't understand the teaching in the Course about "usurping the throne of God." Could you elaborate?

Holy Spirit: You have just experienced healing. Your pain was a direct result of your decision to resist God's Will for you. Your healing was a direct result of your decision to let go and say yes to God's Will for you. It seems to be in the form of a marriage with

David right now. Resisting the marriage, holding onto the past, and engaging in hypotheticals had you in conflict, which is pain. It is this simple.

Resisting God's Will places God outside of yourself. You see yourself as separate from Him. You fear and reject His Love because you think you know better. Then when things don't go your way, you prove to yourself that God doesn't love you. Your pain seems to increase, and reasons outside of yourself, such as the body, are claimed to be causative.

In your sick righteousness, you are your own creator—powerful and all-knowing, able to determine why you are in the uncomfortable state you are in. Your thoughts of pain and separation are death; therefore, your assumed strength and wisdom have proven you right. You sit upon your throne, believing yourself to be all-knowing, when, in truth, your supposed insight has brought you only your mistaken perception of yourself.

Kirsten: Thank you so much. I accept that sickness is a decision and that it always involves my resisting God's Will for me. When I join my will with God's, I am saying I have no use for this. I set both my mind and the world free from guilt and sickness. My mind is causative; the world is not. I will let this learning transfer to all of my experiences. I am filled with a deep feeling of love and peace.

No Compromise

Unfortunately for my parents, when I arrived in New Zealand I was in what I call the "metaphysical Nazi stage," which occurs when someone is so riveted on learning the truth that they feel intolerant of anything that doesn't align with the language and metaphysics taught in ACIM. It's not a particularly joyful or loving state of mind, and it's far from open-mindedness, but it's a phase that most of us go through in our desire to wake up!

I was practicing listening to the Spirit and not engaging with anything that didn't feel authentic to me. Much of the conversation with my father repelled rather than attracted me. I could feel his discomfort. I didn't want to deliberately cause any upset, but I simply couldn't engage in discussions about childhood, traffic problems, and politics. Sometimes I felt so uncomfortable that I wanted to leave the room—which would make him try even harder to connect. I felt so much guilt!

At one point, Jackie angrily burst out, "Kirsten, can't you just speak to your father differently?" I went into prayer, truly willing to do what was most helpful. My two worlds were not meeting. I seemed to have two options: try to interact through a role that I didn't identify with anymore or stay true to the transformation that was happening in my mind. I knew that I didn't actually have a choice, and so I offered to be quiet.

I spent most of the following two days in my room, praying and allowing the healing of my mind. I trusted that somehow it was all going to work out, but I knew I couldn't fix or heal the relationships myself.

In the quiet of my room, memories from my mountain bike accident came to mind. That crash was the permission I had needed to stop running. Although I had experienced a great deal of physical and emotional pain, the hardest part for me to face was the fact that I was no longer able to play the role of helper, healer, and fixer of everyone else's lives. I couldn't be the ideal friend, sister, daughter, employee, or teacher anymore. This was devastating. It was the beginning of the end of the Kirsten who could do everything for herself. Since the age of three, I had insisted on being self-sufficient. After the bike accident, I had to move in with my parents and allow myself to be totally taken care of. With both my wrists broken, they even had to brush my teeth for me! It was a complete undoing of pride and independence.

Additionally, all of my distractions were gone. No longer able to escape from the thoughts and beliefs in my mind or to control the external world in any way, I had no choice but to shift my attention towards inner listening. I started to notice what increased the pain and what felt gentle and nurturing.

Since I was in a position where I was consciously aware that I needed help and was open to receiving it, the Spirit was able to communicate with me directly. This was when my deep, heartfelt prayer for healing began to be answered. A friend gave me a runes guidebook and a bag of rune stones, with which I began to do intuitive readings. I would ask a question about my life and select a stone for an answer. Just having the courage to get in touch with my questions was a very healing step. I could feel my heart opening just by my willingness to turn inward and dare to ask for help. Sometimes I couldn't fully formulate my questions, but it didn't matter—by intuitively selecting stones, the perfect answers would come. I began to realize that something beyond me was doing the choosing, revealing answers to me in a way that I recognized. Through this practice, I felt a growing sense of an inner connection and strength.

I was excited to offer the gift of intuitive readings to friends and family, but when my attention went to helping others, I felt the difference immediately. I felt disconnected, lost in an anxious state of not knowing who I was. For the first time in my life, I was aware that I was to give all of my attention to my own healing. My mind training had begun.

Now, back in my family home again, I still wanted to assure everyone that I loved them by trying to help, fix, and heal our relationships. I could feel the pang of abandonment when I didn't respond to the urge to reach out. But rather than being an "unhealed healer," I turned to prayer, my Course lessons, and Chapter 16 from the Course about True Empathy. T-16.I

The undoing of specialness was occurring, and I trusted Jesus completely. There was no way that I could direct the unwinding from relationships because I was the one being unwound! I continued to surrender to the experience and stay in the simplicity of following one prompt after another as to when to leave my room and when to engage.

During this time, my younger brother was living back at home. His girlfriend would come and stay overnight occasionally. They had a tumultuous relationship, breaking up every week or two. In the early hours of the morning, we would often hear her sports car revving out of the driveway and racing off down the road. My younger brother would be emotionally affected, swinging between feeling responsible for her reactions and being angry at her immaturity. Roger and Jackie advised him to end the relationship and shook their heads over why he would continue to "do this to himself." But the game changed when they found out she was pregnant.

Unable to direct or control the situation, but emotionally affected now that their future grandchild was involved, Roger and Jackie found themselves disturbed by this latest rift, and they came and knocked on my door.

I was in meditation. When I opened the door I felt a soft, open-minded, open-hearted welcome. Roger was in full agreement when Jackie said, "You're the only one who isn't affected, Kirsten. We need your help." I was deeply grateful. Here was the answer to my prayer. By not compromising, and putting the Holy Spirit's purpose first, I was now able to be truly helpful.

Roger, Jackie, and I had a beautiful talk about the concepts of "mother" and "father," and the responsibility, guilt, and pain that are part of these roles. They were more than ready to be relieved of those feelings—after all, my younger brother was twenty-seven years old! Later that week, I found myself sitting with my brother and his girlfriend, drawing the "right mind" and the "wrong mind" out on paper and helping them identify what it felt like to be in each one. Our joining became a workshop that I later shared with the Course group. Again, I was being shown how loving God's plan truly is.

Stop, Drop, and Roll

There were times when I found myself unsure of what to do with a repetitive thought pattern. Sometimes it felt like a meaningless distraction, and at other times inner inquiry would lead to genuine healing. Friends asked me for advice on this and it was hard to give an answer that felt applicable for every situation.

The Holy Spirit gave me a great catch-phrase: "Stop, drop, and roll." It is what firefighters say to do if you catch on fire, or you're surrounded by smoke and you can't see straight. It is the perfect thing to do in an emergency!

1. Stop following the thoughts.
2. Drop down to a place where prayer is possible.
3. Roll with the Holy Spirit—that is, feel the peace and ask for guidance.

If further help is needed: Acknowledge that you don't know why you feel this way, but that you are willing to be guided as to what to say, and do now. When you have a quiet time to yourself, bring the feelings up again with the Holy Spirit and ask about them. Anger always seems justified in the moment, but when tracked much deeper, there is always a hurt underneath and an unseen belief to uncover.

A Visa Miracle

I had a visa appointment in Auckland city at the U.S. Embassy, and I set my alarm for the following morning in preparation, allowing plenty of time for the rush-hour traffic. I was shocked when I awoke and realized that my alarm had not gone off. Jackie, who was accompanying me, had also slept in. We couldn't believe it. We were quickly in the car and joining in prayer. I felt fear arising, as we were leaving an hour later than we'd planned—we would need a miracle to arrive at the Embassy in time!

There was no time for doubt thoughts, and we focused our minds completely on the miracle, giving the whole situation over to Jesus. We noticed the traffic was unusually light, but stayed in prayer, thinking that at any moment we would be hitting a traffic jam. I read through a few of my journal writings and reminded myself that this appointment was simply another opportunity for holy encounters. I didn't have to say the right thing or convince anybody of anything.

Each time we rounded a corner or came over a rise we expected to see an ocean of red brake-lights ahead—but they never appeared! It was more like the scene in the movie *Vanilla Sky* when Tom Cruise goes running through the empty city streets.

We sailed down the motorway, and at the final approach to the city we whooped with delight. It was a miracle! We were twenty minutes early! Jackie sent me in for my appointment with a beaming smile. This was bigger than just a traffic miracle; this was confirmation of the entire awakening journey for us. I knew now that I was definitely to apply for this visa and to be based in the U.S.

Everyone at the Embassy reflected my miraculous state of mind—the guard on duty was happy, the interviewers were sweeties, and the children waiting with their parents kept me amused with clapping and singing games. Within ten minutes I was told that my passport would be sent to me within the next day or two with a religious visa that would give me up to five years in the U.S. I heard later that Tiger Woods happened to be playing golf in Auckland that morning—it seemed that half of Auckland's population had stayed home to watch him play!

I returned to the Peace House on the wings of love. Even though my family wanted me to stay in New Zealand and hoped that I would return soon, it was clear to all of us that returning to the States was the direction for me.

Not long after I returned, David and I were invited to visit with friends from the online ACIM-Gather group in California. I was about to realize that I had an addiction!

Chapter Seven
Sleep versus God
Summer 2005

"This world is full of miracles. They stand in shining silence next to every dream of pain and suffering, of sin and guilt. They are the dream's alternative, the choice to be the dreamer, rather than deny the active role in making up the dream. They are the glad effects of taking back the consequence of sickness to its cause. The body is released because the mind acknowledges 'this is not done to me, but I am doing this.' And thus the mind is free to make another choice instead." T-28.II.12

Sleep Addiction

David and I were invited to California by some ACIM friends to hold a few gatherings. Our friends' dogs barked during the first night, and I was woken up several times. I worried about how my energy would be the following day. I consoled myself that I could always take a nap in the afternoon if needed. The following night I expected to be very tired, but found instead that I couldn't sleep. I remembered that I had drunk a cup of coffee around lunchtime—no wonder! Caffeine kept me up if I drank it after midday. I spent most of the night meditating and wishing that I hadn't had that cup of coffee.

The following night I was so ready to drift off that I expected to go right to sleep. It was 10 p.m., and I counted how many hours I would get if I slept straight through to morning. I was so happy at the thought of getting a good night's sleep! However, David and I were in twin beds in the guest room, and as soon as his head hit the pillow he began to snore! It was soft snoring, but nevertheless I put my earplugs in, trying to shut out the noise. They didn't work at all. By this time I was highly concerned about having had hardly any sleep for two nights straight. As the hours ticked by I counted along with them, worried that I would suffer the next day.

I had eventually fallen asleep in the early hours of the morning. When David woke in the early morning, as usual, his movements woke me. I was not ready to be awake and so I tried very hard to go back to sleep. It didn't work, and I felt resentful towards David.

The dogs were active again the following night, and then a house alarm went off, and on it went. Each night I would put in my earplugs, trying to protect myself from an external world that was against me. Feeling like an overtired victim stuck in a situation that I had no control over, more attack thoughts arose: *Why do these people have so many dogs? It's ridiculous. They say they are rescuing them, but they're just locked up in a backyard, barking at everything that moves—it's cruelty, not kindness!* I felt utterly trapped: trapped in my mind, in the room, in a situation that was not my choice.

Feeling trapped in a noisy world was not new to me. When I was recovering from my head injury at Jackie and Roger's house, I had experienced an extremely high sensitivity to noise. So many sounds bothered me—lawn mowers, airplanes, even the sound of a car door closing.

I remember opening *A Course in Miracles* for the first time. I opened the book at random, and the first thing I read rocked my world. I immediately knew this was the answer to the deepest prayer of my heart—which was for freedom. It read, "... you have no control over the world you made ... it is made out of what you do not want." T-12.III.9 It went on to say that the world was all within my own mind, and the only control I have is how I perceive it.

I had a sweeping realization that I had always tried to manage my life and my world, and this was why it didn't work. I began to pay attention to the direction of my thinking, and I noticed that I would lie in bed "listening" for what would disturb me! My radar was up, waiting. Sure enough, I would always pick up on something that I felt I did not want to hear!

As I lay in California remembering all of this, I suddenly sat up in bed. I realized that I'd become so lost in my desire for sleep that I'd completely forgotten about Awakening! I grabbed my journal and pen and got down to business with the Spirit. I'd blamed my inability to sleep on over-tiredness, under-tiredness, snoring, dogs, caffeine, etc., but now it was obvious that the only consistent factor in all of this was me! It was time to get honest! I was ready to go deeper.

I sat in prayer and opened my mind completely to the Spirit. I felt a gentle calmness envelop me that I had not felt for over a week. What had I been doing? How could I have forgotten to ask for help?

Journaling

Kirsten: Holy Spirit, help me to see what is going on. What do I believe about sleep?

I began to write. The writing flowed from my pen as each belief was clearly seen, appearing within my mind as clear as day.

• I believe that I need a certain amount of sleep.

• I believe that I need a certain quality of sleep.

• I believe that if I don't get the right type and amount of sleep, I will be tired the next day, possibly head-achy, and probably unable to feel energetic and happy. In other words, my health depends on my sleep.

• I believe that when I'm asleep, I'm at peace.

• I believe my sleep can be disturbed by something that seems to be happening in the world.

• I believe that I am kept awake, and that my precious sleep is disturbed or taken from me on a regular basis.

• I believe that I'm at the mercy of a world outside of myself, and that I am a victim.

Wow! I knew I had a thing about sleep, but not that I had such an intense special relationship with it! *I really believe that my health depends on sleep.* Holy Spirit, what is health?

Holy Spirit: Health is in the mind, not the body. To try to fix a problem at the level of the body makes the problem seem real. When solutions in form are sought, there is always a feeling of powerlessness, of vulnerability, of being at the mercy of the outside world.

Kirsten: Believing that I need a certain amount and quality of sleep to be healthy and happy leads to my feeling attacked and believing that my peace is disturbed. I've gotten into the habit of using earplugs often and now they seem like attack thoughts! I put them in hoping that they* will protect me from a disturbing world. Sometimes they work, other times they don't.

Holy Spirit: All forms of magic work "sometimes." The healing is not in them, and when you become dependent on any form of magic, you make your perceived problem real.

Kirsten: I have read in the Course that this is all a dream, that there is no difference between my waking dreams and my sleeping dreams. Although I am willing to believe this, I can't quite grasp it. I know the Course says that I am shifting from a nightmare to a happy dream. Therefore, the idea of being "woken up" from sleep in this world should be something to look forward to, rather than being something I am disturbed by. Ahh ... only the ego would be disturbed by that! Spirit has no need of sleep.

Okay, I get it. Anything that seems disturbing has to be ego misperception. I am not a victim. I am not at the mercy of the world. I will not play this game any more. Goodbye, need for sleep, I'm done with you. I give this to you, Holy Spirit. I know that perfect health is a state of mind. The belief in sacred sleep has kept me in prison for so long, and now the door is unlocked. I'm free!

[It dawned on my mind that who I am as Spirit never needed sleep. I felt a profound shift. It was a shift of identity, from the one in need of sleep who was asking the external Holy Spirit for help, to knowing the Holy Spirit within as a present experience. Finally, at 4:30 a.m. I fell into a deep sleep. The next day I awoke with what felt like a full-blown flu. It lasted for less than twelve hours, which didn't surprise me since I'd exposed the beliefs that were keeping me in darkness.]

More on Sleep

Journaling

Kirsten: Good morning, Holy Spirit. I had another sleepless night. Although I thought I had let go of the above beliefs, I still feel that I am kept awake or get woken up before I am ready, and this is mostly projected onto David. Please help me with this perception. I must be holding onto beliefs of victimization to still be bothered by this.

Holy Spirit: You believe there are real causes and effects within this world. You lie in bed "awake" and then look for a cause for the effect you believe you are experiencing.

Kirsten: Help me to understand the purpose I am giving the world.

Holy Spirit: Suffering is the experience of blaming your brother for what you believe he did to you. Suffering and sin are reflections of their false cause, which is separation. You believe your brother is separate from you, that there is a world outside of you, and that there are many causes in the world that can disturb your peace. This places you at the mercy of a world that is separate from your mind. This is not so. You are the dreamer of the dream. Your brother represents his Father, your Father.

Kirsten: Yes. "As you see him you will see yourself … in him you will find yourself or lose yourself." T-8.III.4

Holy Spirit: You can choose to perceive your brother as offering you either life or death, as God offering you either life or death. Remember always, God gives only life.

Kirsten: When I'm lying in bed at night unable to sleep, and when I'm in pain, feeling disturbed—focusing on the cause of my disturbance and wishing it was different—I am simply witnessing the belief in separation. I am choosing death instead of life. I am dreaming pain instead of joy. I am holding onto a war that I created for myself, and the purpose that the ego gave the world is being fulfilled. I guess the question to ask myself is, "Would I rather be right or peaceful?"

Holy Spirit: Let go of the nightmare. Rest in me. Thank your brother for offering you life. In him you will find pain or peace, death or life, Heaven or hell. The choice is simple and easy to make now that you are aware of what it is. Let my dreams of forgiveness replace the dream of separation. Let a happy dream replace the dream of guilt; let a peaceful dream caress your mind as the nightmare fades from your awareness. God wills that you awaken gently to the awareness that you have never left His loving arms.

Read Workbook Lesson 351: "My sinless brother is my guide to peace. My sinful brother is my guide to pain. And which I choose to see I will behold."

How to Remember God

Journaling

Kirsten: Why would I make up memory?

Holy Spirit: To take the place of what God gave you. You really believe that you killed your Father, that you separated from Him. Attempting to recreate a home, a pseudo place of safety, was when memory came to be used. It is simply another layer, another cover over the truth, another wisp of denial of who you are. Give your memories to me and let me reinterpret them for you.

Kirsten: Why can't I remember God? I try to have a mental picture, and it seems so far away from my awareness.

Holy Spirit: The closest you can come to remembering God while believing in a world of form is feeling, or experiencing God. All memories in this world are pictures, forms, images of objects, people, places, times, and events. God cannot be remembered in these terms, as God is not limited to form. The feeling you experience when you are in love, when you are joined with Me along with your brother or sister in a moment of truth, when love floods your awareness, and all you feel is joy, wholeness, completion—this is like a reflection of God's Love.

Kirsten: What do you mean by a reflection? Again, I have ideas of what reflections are in this world.

Holy Spirit: Reflections of God's Love are experiences. Try not to think in terms of images and pictures, since these are perceptual rather than experiential.

Kirsten: How about in meditation? I often experience a feeling of peace, oneness, and stillness.

Holy Spirit: Meditation is giving yourself the opportunity to leave the world of images and form, of emptying the mind of all the thoughts and busyness that distract you from the present moment. It allows you to sink into the deep, restful part of your mind where communication with Me, the voice for God, is possible. Communication here is often without words, as words are symbols used in the world of form. The experience of peace, oneness, and stillness is communication.

Kirsten: Sometimes during meditation I feel as if I'm literally resting in the arms of God. You have used these words often while helping me try to remember the truth.

Holy Spirit: Yes, remember that words are symbols. God doesn't have arms, but while you still believe in and see images in form, the symbol of being in God's loving arms is a comfort to you. I am here as your Comforter, using all of the symbols that you are familiar with as signposts or metaphors to guide you back to your awareness of God.

Cause and Effect

This morning I found myself in study mode with the Holy Spirit, reading and taking notes from the Course: Chapter 28, "The Undoing of Fear."

Journaling

Kirsten: The Course teaches that the dream reflects the belief that I separated from God and that because I fear God, the figures in the dream seem fearful. What can you tell me about this?

Holy Spirit: Know that you are the dreamer, that you actively dream the dream. The world reflects the thoughts and beliefs within your mind. Remember Me always. When I am the guiding light within your mind in every moment, you are remembering God because I hold the memory of God always. You are asleep in the sense that you have turned away from God in fear. When all fear of God has left your mind, you will Awaken.

Kirsten: I don't really think I fear God—I didn't even know God in this lifetime until two years ago. Why do you say that I fear God? What does it look like in this world? [I experienced feelings of nervousness and fear welling up.]

Holy Spirit: This world, the dream you are dreaming, plays out your fear in form. Since you believe, or dream, that you deprived your Father of his Son, you dream of deprivation and separation. This world plays out that fear. You believe that you are the cause of your existence, that you can create your own life, and that you have experiences within this world—some of which you choose, and some that happen to you. This is a backwards and utterly untrue perception.

Kirsten: It seems like a struggle this morning. I've written and crossed out several sentences. Why is this?

Holy Spirit: Your resistance is high. When you really understand the concept of cause and effect, of true Cause and Effect versus false cause and effect, you will see this world for what it is. Right now you are having glimpses. Confusion produced this dream. When you have cleared your mind of all confusion, you will be free of the dream.

Kirsten: What would be helpful to keep in mind right now as I continue to learn and apply this?

Holy Spirit: Remember that God loves you!

Kirsten: Thank you, Holy Spirit. I am eternally grateful for your gentle, loving guidance.

Mystical Experience at the Lunch Table

David and I were called to be on the road a lot, and we put out a silent prayer for support. Regina contacted us, saying she'd found David's teachings on the Internet and had heard specific guidance from the Spirit to steward the ministry while we were traveling. It was another miraculous demonstration of how the Spirit takes care of everything!

We drove to Regina's home in North Carolina to spend some days together as we trained her for the handover. Regina and I got into a rhythmic flow of making several hundred new CDs and DVDs for her to distribute over the coming months.

I noticed that although I had hardly slept over the past few nights, I felt highly alert. During the night I didn't know if I was meditating, sleeping, or awake, and it didn't matter. I didn't judge it, and I felt wonderful. I had an abundance of energy throughout the day. I shared with David that I used to associate a feeling of deep peace and delicious drowsiness with falling asleep. I used to crave that feeling. Now I could see that feeling was part of the special relationship I had with the concept of sleep—it didn't mean anything. David was delighted with my discovery, sparkling as he did, upon hearing my insights.

One day as Regina and I worked, I was in an experience of "no thought"—feeling the effortless and joyful flow of immersing ourselves in the Spirit's purpose.

At lunchtime I sat down at the table, and in the next moment all sense of a "gap" completely disappeared. I was in the experience of Oneness; everything was connected. I was in the midst of knowing that love is all there is. The presence of love extended everywhere and included everything. It was all One Self.

Everything was very bright and vivid, particularly the food on my plate. I looked down and there was the most beautiful red tomato I had ever seen! I lifted my sandwich but couldn't comprehend putting it in my mouth. The arms in front of me didn't seem like part of me at all, and it felt like there was no stomach to receive the food. Slowly I lowered the sandwich back down onto the plate. The awareness of love, like a white cloud, filled the room and then spilled out into the hallway. I could feel it extending through the rest of the house, and then outside to everything, everywhere.

David and Regina were near me, and tears began running down my cheeks as I shared a few words of what I was experiencing. They sat there nodding at me with their eyes shining. I felt like a child, hardly able to speak, not knowing what I looked like, or sounded like, or if I would be understood. I felt tenderly vulnerable, but at the same time the experience was so beautiful, and so safe.

Later in the day we went for ice cream, and I had the experience again. I was eating ice cream with "me," but it was me in the form of David, Regina, and Regina's daughter Jasmine. I delighted at the awareness of how adorable I was.

Chapter Eight
Carried from Darkness to Light

Summer 2005

"There can be no salvation in the dream as you are dreaming it. ... Little child, the light is there. You do but dream, and idols are the toys you dream you play with. Who has need of toys but children? They pretend they rule the world, and give their toys the power to move about, and talk and think and feel and speak for them. Yet everything their toys appear to do is in the minds of those who play with them." T-29.IX.4

"Forgiving dreams have little need to last. ... And in these dreams a melody is heard that everyone remembers, though he has not heard it since before all time began." T-29.IX.8

Letting Go of the Fearful Dream

This morning I read "The Forgiving Dream" in the Course. T-29.IX As I read, it was like watching a television program and seeing a child playing with toys in a game that has gone horribly wrong. Watching from the perspective of a loving parent, I can see that it is just a child's game. However, the game and the fear seem so real that the child does not know how to stop the game and walk away.

To know that my life is like a child's game, and that I am giving all of the toys their roles and their reactions to play, is amazing. It's not frightening when I know that I am the dreamer of the dream, the maker of the game. The game is only continuing to be played because I want it to continue—and that gives it a totally different perspective. In this remembrance, I am no longer at the mercy of an external world. I can choose to end the game at any time by refusing to play, by walking away.

I have made the decision that it is time to let childhood pass. I forgive my dream and myself. I am safe.

I Am a Thought in the Mind of God

Journaling

Kirsten: Good Morning, Holy Spirit. I read in the text, "Decide for truth and everything is yours" and "Decide for idols and you ask for loss." T-30.III.1 Can you tell me more about this and tie it in with how I am a thought in the Mind of God?

Holy Spirit: The Mind of God is unlimited, whole, and complete. You are a thought in the Mind of God—unlimited, whole, and complete. Your thoughts, including the Thoughts of God, are forever in your mind, as ideas leave not their source. You can obscure the Thought of God from your awareness, but this does not mean that anything has changed. God's Love is eternal, changeless, and unaffected by your forgetting.

Love is *always* here right now. But your awareness of Love's presence is not. In the parable of the Prodigal Son, the father "ran and embraced him." (Luke 15:20) This is a metaphor for His son turning around and remembering what is forever true. God is. This will not and cannot ever change. God cannot leave. God cannot forget His Son. How could wholeness and completion be apart? There is nowhere else for them to go! Eternity is everything everywhere.

When the holy Son of God forgets the simple fact that he is whole and complete, he tends to look for completion and wholeness where it is not.

Kirsten: When an idol, or substitute for God's Love, dies—including the end of a relationship that I believe made me whole and complete—I feel like part of me has died. My belief in loss is made real, suffering is made real, and my world is a painful place to be. Love then seems to involve pain and loss.

It keeps coming back to "Seek Not Outside Yourself." T-29.VII The process of letting go of all special relationships is clearing every scrap of everything that I hold onto, everything that I am afraid of losing. I give all of my relationships to you, Holy Spirit. I desire only love. I don't want to hold onto anything that involves pain and potential loss. It's what makes me feel afraid of the future and unable to be immersed fully in the present moment—the only place where the remembrance of God is possible.

Holy Spirit: Amen

Be the Observer and Enjoy the Play

After our time with Regina, handing over the ministry functions, David and I were back at the Peace House for a couple of weeks to rest and prepare for our upcoming trip.

Journaling

Kirsten: Good morning, Holy Spirit. I enjoyed watching the movie *Deconstructing Harry* last night. It clearly showed that the main character made up all the people in his life based on his perceptions of them. I see that I too create all of the characters in my life, and my perceptions of them are what makes them seem separate from me. When I have expectations of them, I give them a purpose other than forgiveness; I bind myself to my beliefs and to the world. In the "deconstructing Kirsten" process, it is clear that I have to acknowledge and release all of my beliefs about the identity I've given everyone, including myself. Last night a new friend who's visiting shared his experiences of being "the observer." He asked, "How can I stay in that experience?"

Holy Spirit: Rather than spending time asking "who, what, when, where, and why," just accept the simple fact that this is all made up. It's that simple. You give everything you see—yourself and everyone around you—roles and identities. Give me all your ideas about it, and I will reinterpret them for you. Come watch the play with me; we have the best seats in the house! From a place of safety high above the stage, the play is very joyful. You know the characters well; you know the actors intimately. You see your beloved ones performing for you as if on opening night.

Sometimes the characters weep with sorrow, then they laugh and burst with song. As the play ends, the characters take a bow. Those who seemed to have lost and mourned are there, bowing with those who seemed to have rejoiced. The actors look up at you; their eyes are shining with love. They applaud you in gratitude for viewing from on high, and for allowing them to fulfil the roles you've given them.

You've forgotten that you are the scriptwriter, that you assigned the roles. In your forgetting, you have joined the characters on the stage, trying in vain to direct the play from a place of concern and despair. When you did this, you gave the characters reality, thus making the stage a frightening battleground. In remembering the truth about your Self, you can see it for what it was—a stage act.

Enjoy your freedom as surely as the actors are enjoying theirs— eternally grateful to remember who they are, no longer caught in a play that was given reality for a moment. The questions that puzzled the characters have disappeared. None of them matter now that the truth has dawned.

The final curtain comes down in front of the happy cast. As the curtain is raised again, the stage is clear, and a reverent peace fills the air. The characters have completed their roles. The actors have come to sit with you—healed and whole in the remembrance of who you are. You sit together as one, basking in the joy of completion. It is done.

False Forgiveness

Journaling

Kirsten: Good morning, Holy Spirit. Fear has been arising. I think I can see the reason I have the fear, after reading about true and false forgiveness in the text. Do you have some words to help me through the fear?

Holy Spirit: Say, "When I am afraid, I am perceiving attack. Attack is impossible, and so I must be perceiving wrongly. Who is attacking me? I am. There is no one outside of myself; therefore, there is no one to attack me. I have made this attack seem real. I am willing to practice true forgiveness because all I want is peace."

Kirsten: Thank you.

Holy Spirit: Give your fears to me.

Kirsten: I thought I had, but I still feel stressed. Why?

Holy Spirit: Can you recall incidents where you offered false forgiveness? You pardoned your brother for what you believe he did to you. It is this that keeps the fear hidden, and it seems difficult to expose. Think of a time when you have spoken about an incident when your brother hurt you or pushed you or made you feel uncomfortable.

Kirsten: Got it! I remember a time—and it came up again recently, too—when I perceived that David was pushing me beyond my comfort zone. He made me face a situation and go through it when I felt I wasn't ready, and it's happening again now. I am willing to be wrong about this. I have made this attack seem real, and all I want is peace.

Holy Spirit: David reflects part of your mind; that is all. His thoughts reflect your own thoughts, but you are not willing to admit this at times. Your readiness and willingness to let go and move forward is a direct reflection of your peaceful state of mind. Hold on to any idol and you are resisting God's Will for you.

Kirsten: I know it's of the ego when I want to do it my way, in my own time, when I'm good and ready. There's a feeling of separation that goes with the thought of not wanting to do something "because David said so," as if "he" is separate from "me." I know his thoughts are my own; I have them before he voices them. Yet I still react with defense when he speaks the words that I have repressed. It's crazy.

Holy Spirit: How are you feeling now?

Kirsten: The fear has gone! David is innocent. Thank you, thank you, thank you! I'm going to have a peaceful, relaxing day now.

Holy Spirit: Wonderful.

Anger and Wrong-Mindedness

I was guided to walk to the post office while listening to "Going Deeper," a talk of David's from the 1990's. Listening, I realized that David and Beverly, the student he was talking with, were describing the experience I was having. They talked about perceiving the environment outside as being disturbing to peace of mind. I was feeling disturbed by a noisy vehicle driving past! In fact, I couldn't even hear the dialogue and had to pause and rewind the audio. As they talked further about this misperception, I became more and more irritated—noisy vehicles continued to go by, the sun grew increasingly hot, and a *very* long train rumbled past. *Grrrrrr* ...

David was talking about the subject/object split. Yes! Clearly there was a subject/object split going on in my mind. As this awareness dawned, my irritation peaked. I was overheating, my MP3 player came unhooked and crashed to the sidewalk, and I'd had to continually stop the audio and wait for noisy vehicles to pass by. I couldn't believe what was happening. It took everything I had to focus my mind on what David was saying, and in the exact moment that Beverly came to the realization that she could be disturbed only by her thoughts, the world seemed to come to a gentle pause for me.

I stopped and handed everything over to the Holy Spirit. My vision changed, and for a few moments I experienced oneness with everything around me. I was flooded with the awareness that there was nothing outside of my mind that could possibly disturb me. A peaceful hush fell upon the world, and I was delighted to find myself walking in cool shade all the way back to the Peace House. What an amazing healing!

Carried from Darkness to Light

Journaling

Kirsten: Good morning, Holy Spirit. This morning I awoke feeling tired and irritable. Help!

Holy Spirit: Read Lesson 6, "I am upset because I see something that is not there."

Kirsten: Well, yes. There is nothing that I can see that is the cause of my annoyance, but I feel annoyed. I have tense shoulders and an unsettled stomach. *I close my eyes. Peace washes over me and I am serenaded by the Holy Spirit.*

Holy Spirit: [Singing in a beautiful baritone voice with full instrumentals]: "Love is in the air, every time I look around. Love is in the air, in every sight and every sound. It's something that I must believe in, and it's there when I look in your eyes ..."

Kirsten: [Tears well up.]: Oh, I am so loved. Earlier I'd read, "There are no small upsets, they are all equally disturbing to my peace of mind." W-5.4 I will regard this upset as the same as all upsets, and I will let it go. This morning I felt separate to David and Tripod in this state of mind, refusing even to say good morning because I didn't want to. I had a feeling of stubbornness and the thought, *I'm doing my thing, don't interrupt me.* I fed the cats before sitting down but ignored Tripod's request to be let into the basement to play. I decided she could just wait. Humph. It's all ego. Separation. Wrong-mindedness. That's all it is. Is there anything else, Holy Spirit?

Holy Spirit: Remember this is all voluntary. You do not have to "do" anything. The ego will have you feeling pressured and tired, as if you have so much to do and not enough time. With this comes a feeling of sacrifice and then you wish you were elsewhere or doing something else.

Kirsten: Yes. And add to that comparisons and resistance to the future. I compare now with a time when I could meditate and rest all day, and then I don't want to go off travelling without resting first. I have long lists of things to do, phone calls to make, supplies to check and organize, etc.

Holy Spirit: Give your list to me. Ask me what I would have you do. I know your highest good. I will direct you in such a way that your day will flow, and all that needs to be done will be done without the least bit of exertion from you. It is when you look back from a place of wrong-mindedness that you perceive what you are doing as hard work. That belief is then projected onto today, creating a sense of strain.

Kirsten: Yes. When I'm in this place I just can't see the truth. Yesterday when I was in my right mind, everything flowed miraculously. So much was accomplished. It amazes me how twisted it all gets when I'm "in the ego."

Holy Spirit: How are you feeling now?

Kirsten: Much better. I've just noticed a beautiful, new red leaf on that plant.

Holy Spirit: Welcome to your day.

Kirsten: I just remembered to set the tone for my day. I am deciding to have a happy, fun, peaceful day. I feel clear again. I am soooooo grateful. Thank you, Holy Spirit, thank you so much.

Guide to Peace

"My sinless brother is my guide to peace. My sinful brother is my guide to pain. And which I choose to see I will behold." W-351

I read the "Changeless Reality" section from the text this morning, and was inspired to write. T-30.VIII

Journaling

There is nothing outside of my mind.
To judge my brother is to judge myself.
To love my brother and see his innocence
Is to know myself.

This world was projected to hide the thought of terror,
to project sin onto my brother,
to protect the ego by holding onto the belief in sin.

The Holy Spirit is with me always.
I choose to hear His voice
and only His voice,
being the Voice for God.

For the past several months I've been living with a subtle tension, a feeling of sacrifice, as though something is being given up. David is a constant reminder to me of the singular decision for God, so sometimes just being around him increases the tension. Last night it all came pouring out. It felt very strange because although tears were streaming down my cheeks, it didn't feel like it was me who was crying. I felt as if I was observing the character of Kirsten.

I'd been pulling away from David and spending time in a different room, but as my emotions started to arise, he came in right on cue and held me. I allowed everything I was feeling to arise and be spoken out loud; feelings of sadness and loss, thoughts about not knowing who I am, or what to tell my family.

It felt like a complete dismantling of the self-concept. I realized on a deep level that my life was no longer my own. There was no other life I could have. I was no longer who I had been, but I didn't know how to be someone else.

I felt like I was being squeezed through the eye of the needle. The tears flowed, and then before I knew what was happening, a giggle came to replace my sadness. I was on the other side.

Chapter Nine
Choose Wisely

Summer 2005

"How simple is salvation! All it says is what was never true is not true now, and never will be. The impossible has not occurred, and can have no effects. And that is all." T-31.I.1

I Am All Living Things

I read this morning about salvation in "The Final Vision" from the Course. T-31

Journaling

Kirsten: Good morning, Holy Spirit. In a nutshell, there are two lessons: guilt and innocence. If I teach myself that the Son of God is guilty, the outcome is a world of pain and separation. If I teach myself the Son of God is innocent, that is the real world. In this, I see that all living things will to be whole, and I recognize each call for love as it really is. There are two ways of perceiving the world—as either guilty or innocent—and a world arises from each perception.

Holy Spirit: Yes. It is this simple.

Kirsten: So all I need to do is know that my brother and I are innocent and to see past all "forms" to the love behind them, and respond accordingly?

Holy Spirit: Yes.

Kirsten: And when I am tempted by any idol, I am choosing the lesson of the ego. Then I'm likely to see a world of despair and death?

Holy Spirit: Yes.

Kirsten: I must let all judgment and past associations be washed away in order to experience each moment born anew. And I need to let go of the story and greet my brother as if for the first time in order to experience the real world?

Holy Spirit: Yes. Holding onto stories of the past is holding onto a world that you no longer want.

Kirsten: That is false empathy, isn't it? Reminding my brother of his stories makes them seem to be his reality.

Holy Spirit: Binding your brother to the past is sentencing him to death. Releasing him from bondage releases you from your false perception of him. You made this world from your belief that the Son of God is guilty.

Kirsten: No wonder idle chitchat feels like death! There's something else on my mind. Tell me about the line, "There is no living thing that does not share the universal Will that it be whole ..." T-31.I.9 What is a living thing? People and animals come to mind, but it feels like there's more to it.

Holy Spirit: God is life. Life creates in the likeness of life. All of the "things" in this world that you are thinking of are form. They are not life in and of themselves. The Love of God is eternal and all encompassing. The universe perceived with guilt is experienced as a world of death. Perceived with innocence and love, it is experienced as a world in which there is no death. The universe is whole. All living things are one. It is only fragmented perception, a split mind, or a mistaken belief that sees a world of separation.

[I found the above reply from the Holy Spirit difficult to receive; it felt fragmented and scrappy. I scribbled it all out because I wasn't sure it was from the Spirit at all. I later read it through with David and realized that it was from Spirit, but that I was receiving it with a fragmented mind.]

Kirsten: I am all living things!

I've Become a Factory Worker!

"Understand that you do not respond to anything directly, but to your interpretation of it. Your interpretation thus becomes the justification for the response. That is why analyzing the motives of others is hazardous to you. If you decide that someone is really trying to attack you or desert you or enslave you, you will respond as if he had actually done so, having made his error real to you. To interpret error is to give it power, and having done this you will overlook truth." T-12.I.1

The ego was rearing its head as I was in the office stamping CDs for our travels. The task felt beneath me. Burning the CDs, printing the labels, stamping them onto the CDs, putting the CDs into envelopes, and putting rubber bands on one set of CDs after another felt monotonous. Aghhhh! I felt my pride coming up, along with a disdain for the project. I used to be important! Does David have any idea who I am and what I'm capable of? Here I am downstairs stamping hundreds of CDs like a factory worker while he gets to do all of the higher communication functions above me! I resented the project and felt terrible, so I went to see David.

His response? "It's all voluntary. You don't have to do any of it." This was the opposite of what the ego was expecting. I had given David the authority role and me the role of a worker who had no choice but to work hard and obey. I felt a crack of an opening within my mind—like a heavy curtain being pulled aside so a sliver of light could shine into the dark. I remembered that I had volunteered to do this project! Oh, that's right! I had come to the Peace House of my own volition to immerse myself in all of this!

With this recognition I was able to ask David why it felt so "beneath me" to be stamping the CDs. We had a great talk about tasks being used for the sole purpose of undoing the self-concept, including feelings of pride and comparison. David asked if there was something else that I would rather do. I prayed and felt a familiar peace return to my mind. "No!" I happily realized, "There's nothing else that I would rather do than stamp CDs!" I was going through such a deep undoing in my mind that I didn't feel capable of doing anything that involved thinking. Because the CD project was so monotonous and simple, it was the perfect thing to be doing right then!

When I returned downstairs, I felt so much gratitude. The only purpose of the task was the healing of my mind—it was for my relationship with God. And the content of the CDs that I was assisting to make available was so clear and profound. Overwhelmed with gratitude, I ran back upstairs to give David a big hug!

Choose Wisely

"You always choose between your weakness and the strength of Christ in you. And what you choose is what you think is real. Simply by never using weakness to direct your actions, you have given it no power. And the light of Christ in you is given charge of everything you do." T-31.VIII.2

Two years before I met David, I was guided to buy a small house in New Zealand. It feels that the time has come to question the purpose of continuing to own my house. I'm questioning whether or not owning the house is in alignment with Jesus' teachings on divine providence and particularly his question: "The teacher of God does not want anything he cannot give away. … What would he want it *for?*" M-4.VII.2

The last few days have been an emotional roller coaster ride—thoughts of future security, New Zealand, and imagined family reactions all whirling within my mind. This morning I was guided to read "Choose Once Again", which is the very last section of the text. While reading I felt Jesus speaking directly to me.

Journaling

Kirsten: Thank you Jesus. I will not deny you. I will let only strength direct my actions. I will let the power of God direct my actions, my thoughts, and my words. I will share *only* the vision of Christ with my brothers because my strength is theirs. I feel peaceful today, but the house situation is coming to mind. What can you tell me about it?

Jesus: You are concerned about hypotheticals: *What if …? Should I …? Is it better to …? How will Jackie feel? Could there be a better outcome? Can I have both worlds?*

Give the house to me and let it be. Do not follow your actions with doubts. Do not follow meaningless trains of thought based on unknown outcomes in form. Do not doubt your identity. Do not doubt your brother's identity. Do not doubt my guidance. Give everything to me, and follow this action with trust and faith. I will take care of everything in ways that you could not think of because you are coming from a place of doubt. You think you want the best outcomes for everyone concerned, but really you are acting from fear.

Your thoughts are holding you apart from the Will of God. Do not deny me. You deny the gift of the peace of God every time you doubt my guidance. Put all of your faith in me. Put all of your trust in me and keep it there. Do not snatch it back and put it in your own tiny thoughts of fear and lack; they will not bring you what you desire above all else. You hold the power of decision in your hand. Use it wisely. Choose Heaven and it will be given you.

What Am I Really Afraid Of?

As I looked at the idea of selling the house, I felt a fear that seemed out of proportion to the situation; it felt visceral, as if I were actually facing death. I went into prayer to ask why. After all, I was fine before I bought the house, and nothing would actually happen to me physically as a result of selling it. It wasn't as if I were contemplating sky diving without a parachute!

In the quiet of my mind, I realized that the fear thoughts being spoken by my family members were really my own. Projecting onto them was a way to deflect away from seeing that I was the one who was afraid of losing my independence. I saw that the house represented safety, security, and a good investment.

As I sank deeper into my mind, I saw that I was facing the belief that I could make the biggest mistake of all time. It felt as if I were touching on a belief that rippled way back to the first belief—that I could leave God, leave my Home, and lose the only thing that was important—my true safety. My real fear was that I could make an irreversible mistake and would then have to live with the terrible consequence.

I know now that I don't have a purpose for that house other than a false sense of security. Thank you, Jesus. I am so grateful. I want to know that my Home is in God. I trust you.

Delay Is a Defense

Although I now feel clear about letting go of the house, I've noticed my hesitation to announce the news to my family. It feels the same as when I was afraid to tell them that I was marrying David—it was a huge step and a clear sign that my life was going in a completely different direction than any of us had expected.

I remember that I was anxious about facing a reaction of anger or hurt, and I delayed in telling them as a way of "protecting" us all. I realized later that if I'd told them what I was feeling immediately, I could've included them in the adventure. In holding back out of fear, I experienced increased guilt and tension, and it made me feel as if I were stuck between two worlds. The longer I left the communications unspoken, the bigger the risk felt.

As a justification for delaying the inevitable conversation, I had thoughts such as, *They won't understand anyway—how could they? Particularly Roger. He won't understand; he will question me and doubt me.* I would imagine Roger's voice in my mind, expressing all of my doubt thoughts, confirming that he was not in support of the guidance I was receiving.

I recall that my fear of telling my family about getting married had spread to my relationship with David. I had projected my doubt thoughts onto him, as if he were the one forcing me to tell them. I told myself that they weren't ready to hear about my next steps.

I see clearly now that the idea that the present moment is not the right time to communicate only creates a sense of separation that increases the longer I wait. It allows doubt to begin permeating my mind, and a lack of trust in the Spirit then begins to develop. I'm seeing how important it is to communicate directly and without delay. My relationship with God and my whole spiritual journey depends on it.

Chapter Ten
One Lesson—One Mind

Summer 2005

Oneness just Is.
Let go of your ideas
And sink into the experience you Are;
The experience you share with God.

This experience cannot be taught,
nor can it be learned.
Let go of every belief
that holds you apart from your brother

For in him you will find yourSelf.
In him, you will find God.
You and your brother are one,
God has one Son.

The Real Alternative

Journaling

Kirsten: Good morning, Jesus. I have a niggling concern about my family.

Jesus: Be specific.

Kirsten: I don't want them to worry about me. I want them to be happy and to trust that you are my guide.

Jesus: You are speaking of your own happiness and trust.

Kirsten: Yes! I am. There is no compromise when it comes to the truth, but with some things I delay choosing Purpose. I want to hang on a bit longer until it feels like the "timing is right."

Jesus: You want to keep a foot in each world. If you know the only real alternative to illusions is choosing purpose, then you are using timing as a defense against the truth. Let's take a look at the concept of timing.

Kirsten: There is only now. But what about the divine order of things? Synchronicities?

Jesus: Before Abraham was, I AM. Before time began was life eternal. Ask yourself what you are clinging to now that is preventing you from returning to the awareness of Heaven. All pathways in this world lead to death. Right now you are where you seek to be. Right now is all of Heaven within your reach. Right now is all you have ever wanted within you, and the things of this world that you cling to are the blocks to this awareness. Timing is yet another block if you choose to use it as such.

Kirsten: [I laugh with recognition.] Oh, that is so amazingly helpful!

Jesus: Heaven is right here with you, awaiting your joyous return. You are seeking first the Kingdom of Heaven. Keep asking your questions, my innocent child. This is your pathway Home.

The Mask of the Self-Concept

This morning I sat in the sanctuary, feeling stillness and peace radiating out from deep within. Everything was included in it—it extended throughout the room, the neighborhood, the universe. Angel the cat lay sprawled out in her usual position on top of a couch, snoring softly. The fridge was humming, almost crooning, in the background. The song "Silence" by Donna Marie Carey echoed through my mind.

Journaling

Kirsten: Good morning, Holy Spirit. Do you have a message for me?

Holy Spirit: Hold this thought throughout the day, "I am Spirit. I choose to recognize the Spirit. I am worthy that my will be done."

Kirsten: Oh, thank you. Another song floats through my mind—"Holy" by Karen Drucker. "You are holy, holy, holy ... we are holy, holy, holy, we are whole ..." Divine.

I was guided to read "The Savior's Vision" and "Self-Concept versus Self" in Chapter 31 of the Course. It was profound. The awareness that arose from my reading was: Everyone holds a concept of himself, which stands like a shield before the truth. On the surface, this self-concept is "good;" it is the face of innocence, a victim at the mercy of unwanted circumstances. But beneath the surface is the other part of the self, the sense of dark displacement that no one wants to admit is there. This particular line resonated deep within my heart: "The savior's vision is as innocent of what your brother is as it is free of any judgment made upon yourself. It sees no past in anyone at all. And thus it serves a wholly open mind, unclouded by old concepts, and prepared to look on only what the present holds." T-31.VII.13

I felt like celebrating! It's *all* made up! How wonderful! How freeing! And then the depth of this realization struck me. *Oh my God. It's all made up.* Suddenly I saw that every person I'd ever known was a concept. I had feelings of disbelief; I felt like the whole world was being dismantled. Oh, my God. I went to talk to David.

Kirsten: [Tears began to flow.] David, it's just mind-blowing. Everyone I've ever met—my brother, my father, everyone—they are all the face of innocence on the surface, and they are the displaced fearful state that lies beneath. After reading about this in the text, I see why it's no wonder that people can't trust one another. They see the face of innocence and know that there is something else beneath, something hidden. What about the people who are sad, who wish their lives were different, who believe they are abused or victimized? I feel sad for them.

David: If it were true, it would be frustrating and sad. That's why it's so wonderful that there are not individual, separate people. Enlightenment is not individual; it's inclusive. When you accept the Atonement for yourself, everyone is with you. Jesus says that legions upon legions will arise with you, and this is because there is only one experience—only one mind. He goes beyond the concept of separate brothers and sisters in the Workbook Lessons, "When I am healed I am not healed alone" W-137 and "I will accept Atonement for myself." W-139

Kirsten: But what about those who still seem sad or alone? I guess I don't experience this when I'm in my right mind. When I first sat down to study this morning, I was utterly peaceful, and all I experienced for the whole universe was peace and stillness. It's when I see separate people as separate bodies with their own separate minds that I feel sad for some, while others seem fine.

David: There is nothing to be sad about. All the animals that you tried to save as a child were part of the self-concept. You saw the innocent animals, the innocent environment, and the killer humans.

Kirsten: Yes! The innocent faces, the innocent animals ... it was a losing battle. Oh, it's such a relief to see that it's always been my own mind. My head is still spinning a bit.

The following is my understanding from my reading over the past two days: It is freedom to see straight through the masks to true Identity, to the Christ within, to the light. This is my purpose. I am needed for Salvation. It is in laying aside my self-concept and looking upon my brother without the past, without judgment, that I behold the face of Christ. The veil is the fear of God, the belief that there is a gap between my brother and myself. I must believe that I am a separate self in order to perceive this way. The choice I make is Heaven or hell, depending on how I behold my brother and myself. I am Spirit. I choose to recognize Spirit. I desire Heaven, and I am worthy that my will be done.

Transfer of Training

During the night I'd been woken up once again. At the time, I didn't think that I felt disturbed or upset, but I did have the thought that it was unnecessary and could have been avoided.

Journaling

Kirsten: Good morning, Holy Spirit. What can you tell me about my feeling of being disturbed?

Holy Spirit: Read "Choose Once Again" from the text of the Course, and "What is the Real Meaning of Sacrifice" from the Manual for Teachers. T-31.VIII, M-13

Kirsten: Thank you for guiding me to read this again. I know that no one but myself can interfere with my peace, but the subject of sleep is up yet again. Any words of wisdom? I am *so* ready to be done with this!

Holy Spirit: Good. When you tire of an idol and cease to hold it up, which gives it power, it will cease to be.

Kirsten: It's that simple, isn't it?

Holy Spirit: Yes. All strain comes from past and future associations. This trial is a lesson brought to you once more so that you can forgive and release it.

Kirsten: Is there anything else that I'm unaware of? I feel like I've dug and dug and exposed many beliefs involving the construct of sleep, but I still feel disturbed when I am woken up before I'm ready. I always feel like I want more sleep, like I haven't had quite enough.

Holy Spirit: Transfer your training. Apply your learning around "readiness," "being pushed," and "timing" to this construct.

Kirsten: I'm beginning to grasp that the construct of time is deep. Like you told me two days ago, "Before time began was life eternal.

Right now is all of Heaven within your reach. Right now is all you have ever wanted within you, and the things of this world that you cling on to are the blocks to this awareness. Timing/time is yet another block if you choose to use it as such."

My desire for the illusion of sleep keeps it shrouded in mystery for me. It seems normal to expect a certain amount and type of sleep, but these are my made-up beliefs. I am losing peace over them. Not everyone cares about sleep the way that I do; I know it is *my* lesson. I will remember this when I'm tempted to project the cause of my upset onto David and onto time. Anything else?

Holy Spirit: Do what is most helpful, as guided by me, when you are feeling in any way that your peace is being disturbed. I will always direct your actions in a way that joins you with your brother and the truth. Remember always to turn to me. Do not deny me; do not deny yourself the opportunity to return to peace and happiness.

Kirsten: Thank you. I love you.

The Gift of Timelessness

"... time has an ending, and it is this that the teachers of God are appointed to bring about. For time is in their hands." M-1.4

David and I had received many invitations to hold gatherings. When we pieced them all together, we realized that we were about to embark on a seven-month trip! Our stops would include Wisconsin, Vermont, Florida, California, Colombia and Venezuela in South America, and various places in New Zealand and Australia.

Journaling

Kirsten: Good morning, Holy Spirit. Any words for me as we head off on our travels?

Holy Spirit: Demonstrate who you are and what you know: truth, peace, love, oneness. Read from the Course, Who Are God's Teachers? in the Manual for Teachers.

Kirsten: Whenever there is a sense of urgency, stress, or tiredness, it always involves time. What can you tell me about releasing myself from the concept of time? And about having time in my hands as described in the Manual for Teachers?

Holy Spirit: Holding time in your hands is a metaphor. In truth, there is only the holy instant. Eternity knows not of time. Time is a construct, an illusion made up by the ego. Time is of the world—perceived by the body's eyes and experienced by the body and all who believe in it. The effects of time seem to be proven over and over again by every living and dying thing. Everything born in time ends in time. The end of time is cause for celebration indeed! The Son of God cannot die! Your demonstration of who you really are—guiltless, fearless, sinless, peaceful, gentle, trusting, and open-minded—reminds everyone of a love and a life not of this world.

> In this holy instant is God remembered.
> In this holy instant is the world of time forgotten.
> In this holy instant the truth dawns.
> You bring the gift of timelessness with you.

The Truth about Teachers and Pupils

"When pupil and teacher come together, a teaching-learning situation begins. For the teacher is not really the one who does the teaching. God's Teacher speaks to any two who join together for learning purposes. The relationship is holy because of that purpose, and God has promised to send His Spirit into any holy relationship. In the teaching-learning situation, each one learns that giving and receiving are the same." M-2.5

I've been reading and asking about pupils and teachers in the Manual for Teachers during the first days of our drive north.

Journaling

Kirsten: Good morning, Holy Spirit. Please explain, "Certain pupils have been assigned to each of God's teachers, and they will begin to look for him as soon as he has answered the Call." M-2.1 If there is one mind and my brothers are reflections of my Self, how is it they could wait for me?

Holy Spirit: You are experiencing oneness. In reality there are no pupils waiting for their teachers. The instant the thought of separation entered the mind of the Son of God, the Holy Spirit was given. It is done. The Son of God is dreaming of separation. Pupils waiting for their teachers is a helpful metaphor, a symbol for the sleeping mind. The pupils reflect the teacher's willingness, readiness, and trust. The light is in everyone, the mind reaches only to itself. As the doubt—the darkness—is shone away, the light is seen, shining brighter than ever.

Giving and learning are the same. The Spirit enters the mind when any two join together in a shared desire for healing. Time goes backward to the ancient time when it seemed to begin.

Teacher and pupil seem to come together in the present. Metaphorically speaking, when a pupil is desiring truth and divine guidance, he is brought together with one who is also open to receiving and sharing the truth. The one asking the question becomes known as the "pupil." Through their joining, the light shines into their open minds and is recognized as wisdom, truth, or divine guidance.

The Atonement corrected illusions immediately. In time, this seemed to be long ago; *but in reality it never happened.*

Kirsten: So I decide when I want to learn the curriculum. As I accept, it is learned. I get it! Heaven, reality, is deep within. I step back in my mind from the world of time to the truth. It is so clear. Of course! It all makes sense. Where there is an opening, the Spirit flows through because Spirit is everywhere.

Everyone You Meet Is the One

I continue reading from the Manual for Teachers. Jesus describes the "levels of teaching" as different relationship encounters, which fall into one of three categories:

1. Brief encounters, such as meeting in an elevator.

2. More sustained relationships, which are temporary assignments that are maximized when the healing or learning is complete within the relationship.

3. Lifelong relationships, which are assignments that present unlimited opportunities for learning; there can be hostility if the lesson is not recognized.

Journaling

Kirsten: Is the lesson forgiveness?

Holy Spirit: Yes.

Kirsten: So in a lifelong relationship, two people keep pushing each other's buttons and helping to expose the ego in each other. But unless they recognize this and practice forgiveness, the relationship will seem unholy. I understand that salvation is always here because it is always now. Different levels are really just myself, the Son of God, seeming to engage in different relationships to learn "new" lessons, but they aren't really new lessons. The lesson is always forgiveness. I am always meeting a reflection of myself. Every encounter is the opportunity to see the Christ, to lose sight of separate interests and see sameness instead.

Can you explain how the plan includes very specific contacts to be made for each teacher of God?

[I experienced a full understanding from the Spirit, but the communication was not in words. It was an experience. I jotted notes, which are summarized below.]

There is One Mind.

All things are lessons God would have me learn.

All encounters are holy.

There is one decision to make.

I ask for Your guidance and I am brought together with my brother into perfect situations for learning. Every encounter is an opportunity for forgiveness, to see things differently, to see the Christ.

By listening and following You, I am guided as to where to go, who to speak to, and what to say.

Each encounter is holy, a teaching/learning situation in which salvation is present.

The holy instant can be experienced in this purpose; the real world can be seen.

Holy Spirit: Yes. You cannot but be in the right place at the right time. Everyone you meet is the one who offers you salvation. You bring the gift of salvation with you into every meeting and every relationship you experience. Never forget this.

Chapter Eleven
Divine Providence

Summer 2005

"... trust would settle every problem now." T-26.VIII.2

I Feel the Love

David and I drove north to Wisconsin. The trunk of the car held boxes containing the many CDs and DVDs of David's talks that I had made, as well as a portable stereo system for playing songs at the gatherings. The night before we held a small gathering at a friend's home, and it had felt cumbersome to make several trips to the car to carry in the stereo and resources. After we'd carried everything inside, it was my role to set up the resource table and stereo, and of course I wanted to greet our hosts. I felt overwhelmed as people arrived early wanting to connect, and I didn't enjoy feeling rushed and unable to be present with new friends right before a gathering.

We had an evening gathering planned at the Unity Church, and we arrived in the area in the early afternoon. Ready for something to eat we pulled into a parking lot near a McDonald's. We noticed that we'd parked right in front of a luggage store. David suddenly lit up, saying "Perhaps we can find a suitcase to put the resources in." *Wow! What a great idea!* I thought. We both recognized the sweet, easy feeling of the Spirit's direction and happily walked into the store.

A cheerful assistant greeted us, and standing before us were two matching carry-on size suitcases, with wheels and adjustable handles. They were the only ones of that size in the store, and they were on special! We tested the stereo system from the car. It was a perfect fit inside one of the suitcases. The other case was the ideal size for a selection of resources for several gatherings. There would be no more carrying multiple cardboard boxes to and from the car! We were thrilled to have been provided with this simple solution! It was so easy! We shared with the shop assistant what the suitcases were for and how grateful we were to be provided for so lovingly by the Holy Spirit. She totally agreed and sparkled with us, happy to have been part of the miracle!

With our new cases in the trunk of the car we walked into McDonald's, beaming with joy. To our surprise, a voice boomed out across the restaurant as we stepped inside, "I feeeeeel the love! Oh, man, I feeeeeel the love!" We looked up and a beautiful, big, beaming man was looking right at us. We grinned at each other and walked over to him, and he shivered as we walked closer. "Wow!" he said, "You two! What are you doing?! Jesus! I feeeeeel the love from you!" We laughed out loud and had a beautiful encounter with him, reveling in our shared love for Jesus and how amazing this life is!

We arrived at the Unity Church in plenty of time to set up for the gathering, and our new cases worked splendidly!

The Mighty Scoop

I was thrilled with my function of intuitively choosing a song or two to play at the beginning of our gatherings, and one song for the end if there was time. It was also my role to announce the resources table and to speak about donations. That night David held a beautiful, deep gathering. Towards the closing I nervously prepared my speech in my mind. Before I could say a word, however, David spoke. He shared with everyone that we had many, many resources and that it was our joy to give them away for free. His exact words were, "So you just help yourself and take as many as you want, and just leave a donation if you want to."

Right then a woman came running up to the table with a big smile on her face. She lowered her hand in the shape of a scoop, similar to that on the front of a bulldozer, and with one movement she scooped up about twenty CDs. She then whooshed out the door with an ecstatic "Woo-hoo! Thank you so much!"

I couldn't believe it! I looked at David and wondered how he could have said such a thing! All of "my" hard work and not one dollar in the basket! He just looked at me with big shining eyes—the wisdom of the ages quietly amused behind the whole scene. I made my way over to the table, quietly willing to be shown what it was all for.

I could see it. I was being shown how little I knew of divine providence. I could feel the uncertainty each time I was to speak about being supported by donations. All I knew was reciprocity— that you receive something in return for what you give. And if you don't receive, then you don't have. I could tell by the shaky way I talked about being supported by donations that there wasn't a conviction of experience behind my words. My reaction to the woman's "mighty scoop" told me that I believed I'd personally made the CDs, and that we needed a specific amount of funds in relation to those CDs in order to be supported. Later in prayer I realized that I expected to see people giving the same amount, as if it were a cost, in order for me to know that divine providence was working out.

Bumpity House and Ice Cream Miracles

We continued on our journey the following day, and it was a full day's drive to reach our friends Bob and Kathy at their home, "Bumpity House." As we drove up the "bumpity" driveway, Kathy and Bob came outside, climbed on top of a picnic table by the front door, and began singing to welcome us! They were adorable, and in such joy, Bob with his long white ponytail, and Kathy with her soft face and light blue eyes, both singing, "The door is always open and you never have to knock!" I could tell that they meant every word they were singing, and I immediately felt welcome.

We settled in that night, and I was grateful that we had no travels or gatherings planned for two days. *Two whole days*! This was rare, and I looked forward to resting and relaxing with David and my new friends at the spacious property.

The following day I woke up feeling like I had reached my limit. I didn't know why, but I felt a heaviness in my whole being, as if the Spirit had been pulling me and stretching me like a rubber band, and I just couldn't give any more.

David held me in his arms for a while and shared some comforting words about not judging what was coming up or how it looked, and I had a little cry. I couldn't imagine what could help, and I didn't know what to do. David suggested we take a drive. We went into the small, nearby town and came across a park in the town center. We took a walk and then sat on a park bench. I appreciated being alone with David and not being around anyone I didn't know. It felt intense being with new people all the time, and I also didn't want anyone to see me in an ego funk. The feeling just wouldn't shift.

David was loving and supportive, and not at all affected by the darkness that I was in. He seemed as happy as always, and then suddenly he looked up and said, "Look! Dairy Queen!" I didn't know what that was, and it must have shown on my face. "It's an ice cream shop," David explained. I didn't know what I wanted, but I didn't particularly feel like ice cream. "Let's go to Dairy Queen," he said with a smile, as if it were the perfect answer. Feeling hopeless, I obediently stood up, took David's outstretched hand, and walked with him to the shop.

As we walked inside, a little man with a pin-striped outfit and matching red-and-white hat greeted us. David, as if in slow motion, said to him, "Kirsten here is from Neeew Zeeeealand." The little man looked at me and then back at David as he continued, "She has never been to Dairy Queen before. She doesn't even know what Dairy Queen is!" As David spoke, the little man stood up straight and lifted his chest, and by the time David had finished, he was starting to sparkle. He looked at me and said, "You've never been to Dairy Queen before? Well, let me tell you what we have!" He was so animated and joyful to be able to share all about Blizzards, sundaes, and ice cream cones that by the time he was halfway through his list of Blizzards, my mood had completely changed! I was healed by the time we had our ice creams and were walking out the door. The joy of seeing him in his function, sharing his heart, was adorable!

David shared that parable with people everywhere, and word got out that I liked ice cream! Wherever we went our hosts would happily bring out ice cream for me, delighted to offer a gift! Sometimes I really didn't feel like ice cream at all. But the look on our friends' faces as they shared their love with me always touched my heart. I learned to receive the gift of love beyond my personal desire—or lack of desire—in the moment. I was so happy to be part of the gift!

More Lessons on Divine Providence

We had three days of gatherings planned at Bumpity House, and people came from all around Wisconsin. After the first day there was nothing in the donations basket. That night I mentioned it to David. He said, "Oh well, people just give when they feel to." The next day I found myself constantly watching the empty basket. What kind of a demonstration of divine providence was that?! By the end of the second eight-hour day there was still nothing, not even a dollar, in the basket.

Quite a number of people were staying there at Bob and Kathy's, and they gave their donations for their accommodations, but there was nothing coming towards us for the teachings.

That night I felt anger and resentment arising. I watched the thoughts, projected onto all of the participants. *They don't understand the value of what we are giving if they're not supporting it. Nobody values the depth; they don't care; they're just taking for free.* The word "withholding" kept coming to my mind, and I took this deeply into prayer, with a desire to see how I might be withholding.

Immediately I had a flash of New Zealand and my car. I had not given my car over to the Spirit. And then I remembered a bank account. I had a bank account that I was withholding from the Spirit as well. And then I remembered the house in New Zealand that I had not fully given over. All of these possessions were part of a back-up plan if things didn't work out in America. If God's plan for me didn't work out, I had a "Plan B."

For much of the night I went through these areas in my mind, giving them all over to the Spirit in prayer. I allowed the fear of giving them over to rise, feeling like I was brand new again, a babe in Jesus' hands.

By lunchtime the following day I noticed that I hadn't looked at the donation basket once; it had completely left my awareness. I had very little to say and was in a humble, quiet space. My mind had shifted from resentment and lack to a deep sense of honor and gratitude. I remembered that everything that was playing out was helping to show me my mind, my beliefs, and what I clearly still needed to let go of. I no longer had a thought in my mind about money!

During the final afternoon gathering, when David was speaking about trusting in the Spirit for everything, a participant brought up the topic of funds, saying, "Well it's okay for you. You have donations, and you go around with people giving you money, filling your car with gas, taking you in and giving you a place to stay. You are totally provided for by 'everyone else'. And you get paid, so how can you say it's about trust?"

The empty donation basket was the perfect prop to demonstrate divine providence! David responded by holding up the basket and saying, "There is absolutely no obligation or expectation on anybody to have paid anything. Everything is freely given by the Spirit, provided through those who feel the prompt from the Spirit. It all comes from the Spirit." He continued on with a deeply inspiring, beautiful talk on divine providence and how it works—and I knew it was all for me. I shone with deep appreciation and felt so in love with everyone for playing their part so perfectly. After the final gathering, everybody was inspired to give, and the basket overflowed.

I still had a long way to go, but each step was so heavily reinforced with gratitude and abundance that I couldn't miss it. I was experiencing the very real gift of peace of mind and awareness of true safety with every step I took to let go of my fears and need for this world.

Chapter Twelve

I Want to Go Home

Summer/Fall 2005

Love is all there is.
The pathway home to remembrance
Is letting go of everything unlike love.
To remember that Love is all there is,
Is to remember God.
Have faith in the simplicity of the fact
You are that which you seek.
Love is all there is.

Going Home to Heaven

We had a lively discussion one night at Bumpity House in which the subject of "wanting to go home to Heaven" came up. This was my journaling with the Holy Spirit on the following day:

Journaling

Kirsten: Good morning, Holy Spirit. Last night a friend asked, "When will it happen? I want to go home. I want to be in Heaven." As if there really is somewhere else to go. What can you tell me about this?

Holy Spirit: The way you feel right now—peaceful, settled, present— is like being on Heaven's doorstep. This world is made up; its laws are made up. The reason it seems so real and in need of overcoming or escaping is that it was taken seriously. The mind that no longer believes this world to be real and true is free of it. The mind that judges feels trapped in time and space.

Kirsten: The Kingdom of Heaven is within.

Holy Spirit: Yes. The flashes of light and other visual effects that you and your friends experience and talk about are reminders, symbols that this world is not what it seems.

Kirsten: So desiring special effects is not the best use of time. It's better to continue with laying aside all judgment and allowing the transfer of training to take place.

Holy Spirit: Yes. The way to release this world is to let it go. Wishing for and wanting certain experiences in and from it, make it seem real. It is not the world that needs escaping; it is the belief that it is real.

Kirsten: I don't have a driving need to know more than this. I am curious about where to from here, but thinking about it seems to move me away from my one goal, which is the peace of God. Trying to imagine being elsewhere or experiencing something other than what is here and now doesn't feel helpful. It makes time seem real, like an obstacle to heaven, like a real problem between where I am and where I want to be. All I need do is relax and sink into the moment to experience peace; I can feel that this moment is the reflection of the state of Heaven.

Angry at God

Still with our friends at Bumpity House, I went for an afternoon siesta. I found myself become irritated and annoyed as I heard David down the hall brushing his teeth. In my opinion he was making loud and unnecessary noises. Thoughts flew through my mind: *Not everyone makes noises like that. He does it all the time. I'm fed up with this. I shouldn't have to put up with it.* Unsuspecting, David came into the room and lay down. I told him—not for the first time—how I felt. "David, I'm angry at you for making 'hoiking' noises." He replied, "You're not angry with me, you're angry at God," and then he turned over and fell asleep.

I took this in and began to work with it. *I'm angry at God? Why? Because I'm in pain. This world is a painful place. Where is the pain? My head, neck and shoulders have been hurting for two days and now my eyes hurt. If all pain is a decision projected onto the body and this is all my mind, where are my thoughts of pain coming from?*

Taking a mental review of where I'd witnessed pain and suffering recently, I realized I'd been perceiving pain on a daily basis for several days now. One by one, I went through each person and situation where I'd perceived someone to be in pain, struggling with life, or wanting healing but who "wasn't quite there yet." Each time I discovered a memory, I said to myself, "I perceived pain in this person, and I projected this pain onto my body." I repeated this, releasing the pain from my mind and body. By the time I had finished my review all of the pain had gone. Some unspecific sadness came up, and I cried a few tears. But afterwards I felt peaceful. I had been unsure of whether to go out that evening to a movie with David and our friends. Feeling light and free, I got up, showered, and joined them on the outing.

I shared my experience in the car on the way to the movie. Before long, we were all laughing like children in a candy store.

Dreams

Journaling

Kirsten: Good, morning, Holy Spirit. Thank you for this day. My dreams last night were all over the place. Lack of control was the central theme running through all of the different scenarios.

Holy Spirit: Your mind plays out wish fulfillment. Your dreams symbolize your thoughts and your hypothetical alternatives to events that have happened in daily life.

Kirsten: It feels like I'm judging my behavior, my attitude, and myself even in my sleeping dreams. I woke up feeling guilty for telling my dog off in my dream!

Holy Spirit: It's *all* mind, it's *all* thoughts, it's *all* dreams. Give them all to me. Forgive yourself and your perception of what happened, including the characters and their actions. Without purpose, they are meaningless, like everything of this world. Forgive them, give them your blessing, and release them from what you thought they were.

[I sit in meditation and welcome forgiveness to wash through the memories of my recent nighttime dreams and daytime experiences. A gentle peace radiates throughout my mind, blessing everyone and everything.]

Kirsten: Oh thank you, Holy Spirit. I can now see that everything I perceive is my own consciousness. There's a subtle sense that I've done something wrong, that I was dishonest. I want to make amends and get it right "this time" in each dream scenario. I want the world to play the game my way, and I blame the characters if they don't do what I want them to. It's all wrong-minded thoughts, acted out by myself and my characters, based on the belief in separation. I'm trying to control the world based on guilt and fear of lack of control. Do you have anything to add?

Holy Spirit: Love your brother as yourself, including those in your nighttime dreams. You are innocent. Love yourself, including the "you" in your nighttime dreams.

Kirsten: So how about when I set my day? I decide upon the day that I want. I choose peace and love, willing to forgive anything that comes up for healing so that my dream will play out accordingly. After realizing the control issue in the nighttime dreams, perhaps I am also trying to control the daytime dream.

Holy Spirit: The ego perpetuates lack of control and need for control; only the ego does not know what it wants. It decides upon what it wants based on lack and fear, and it tries to control the circumstances and outcomes to have its goal. But it is not satisfied when it gets what it wants. It never feels in control and safe; this is why it craves control, believing it will find security in forms or illusions. When you choose God, you choose to hear and follow my guidance. You are making the one decision that has real results.

In Heaven, there is no lack; therefore, there are no needs. There is nothing missing, nothing to strive for, nothing that could interfere with or limit; therefore control is meaningless.

This world is a stage; the set is full of props. The props will not bring lasting peace and happiness—how can they? They are props! By desiring the props, the characters believe they need to control the play; they fear that the other characters may interfere with the insane desire to attain and keep these hollow objects. When you give your day, your life, to me with total willingness to listen and follow my guidance, I will direct you through this seeming maze of unreal props and scenes. The props can be used as symbols to help point the way for you. Your fellow characters become witnesses to your desire for love, happiness, and peace. When your will is joined with mine, your play becomes enjoyable, filled with miracles, love, and laugher.

Kirsten: Thank you, Holy Spirit.

God's Love

My experience this morning after reading about healing in the Teacher's Manual was the living experience of God—embracing me and surrounding me in the all-encompassing love that is.

I shared my experience with David, Kathy and Bob this morning at Bumpity House. I tried to explain that the love they are and the supportive nurturing environment that comes from our shared purpose *is* the light that shines away the darkness. I've been through a lot of healing in the past two weeks, and it's happened so quickly and easily because every moment I have been showered in love.

Journaling

Kirsten: Good morning, Holy Spirit. This morning's reading said that healing is certain but is not always accepted immediately. So even if I am in doubt, I am to give with trust and certainty of outcome. This is true giving. The Spirit in the mind of the receiver seeks the gift, and it is the Spirit in the mind of the giver who gives it. It is given by God to God: therefore, it can never be wasted, lost, or ineffectual. Do you have anything to add?

Holy Spirit: You give the gift of life to your brother simply by being who you are. Speak to the Christ in your brother. Look not to appearances and temporary illusions that he may hold about himself.

Kirsten: Could you explain "Given by God to God?"

Holy Spirit: God Is. Illusions are nothing. The light, the healing, the love, the truth, and my presence in you, seem to join with your brother when he asks for healing and healing is offered. In truth, there is nothing to heal. This projected world and its images are not the object of healing; the mind is. In truth the mind is healed and whole. When the light shines between two seemingly separate minds, there is a realization that healing is already complete, that there was never really anything to heal. How can what has always been whole be in need of healing? God Is because God is everywhere. God can be felt and experienced, but not seen, in the projected illusions. Moments of intense love and revelations are glimpses of what lies beyond this world.

Kirsten: So healing is simply letting go of the belief that anything of this world is true. Remembering and experiencing God is healing, because it is the truth. There is nothing to heal.

Holy Spirit: Yes.

Kirsten: I can feel His presence now. It seems to be a hum—a gentle and yet powerful, reverent all-ness—surrounding me, embracing me. Home is everywhere. I feel so much gratitude and so much love.

Only the Truth Is True

"The belief in order of difficulties is the basis for the world's perception. It rests on differences; on uneven background and shifting foreground ... on varying degrees of darkness and light, and thousands of contrasts in which each thing seen competes with every other in order to be recognized. ... What the body's eyes behold is only conflict. Look not to them for peace and understanding. ... The one answer to all illusions is truth." M-8.1-6

My morning reading from the Manual for Teachers was on perception. I had some understanding of the teachings, but I also had questions.

Journaling

Kirsten: Good morning, Holy Spirit. I understand the ultimate teaching of the Course—only the truth is true, and only love is real. To have unified perception, the false must all be put in the same category, with no exceptions. Holding onto even one illusion and keeping it apart from the rest is holding on to all illusions. Waking up from this dream means releasing the world entirely. How can I put this into practice?

Holy Spirit: Practice this lesson throughout the day: Put everything you see in one of two categories—true or false, the real or the unreal.

Kirsten: So when I experience love, when I see the Christ in my brother, when I pat the cat and she purrs with happiness ... this is all witnessing to the real?

Holy Spirit: Let's take the scenario with seeing the Christ. The body's eyes may report differences in shape, size, and actions, so these are put in the false, or unreal, category. The experience of the present moment—seeing the Christ, feeling the connection of love between you and your brother—is put in the true, or real category.

Kirsten: The same with the cat? Seeing her body size, various movements, and volume of sounds as differences is the unreal, and enjoying the bliss of present moment together is the real?

Holy Spirit: Yes. For example when you're at the store, seeing the carts, the lights, and the different forms of people is all unreal. Your state of mind—being the present moment, connecting with your brothers, and seeing only the truth of who they are—goes in the category of real.

Kirsten: Great! I have an assignment. Sounds like fun and the perfect way to spend my last day at Bumpity House.

All day I silently put my thoughts into the categories of true or false. Walking outside, I noticed the big tall trees and sighed with happiness. But "big," "tall," and "trees causing happiness" all went into the category of false. So what was my happiness caused by? I paused and felt it—being in the moment was true.

I noticed the light shining through the branches and continued on in appreciation. It didn't feel right to designate this as false, although I knew somehow that the sunlight itself couldn't cause happiness. But something about appreciating the warmth and the light felt good. I continued to walk further and saw a cage. My first thought was a judgment; I was hoping that an animal wasn't caged up. *I won't like our hosts if an animal is caged!* Immediately I placed the thought of a caged animal into the category of false, and noticed my mind shift from concern to feeling inquisitive. Perhaps there was an animal to visit with!

Back at the house I observed my reactions and responses to conversations, people, sounds, and situations. I noticed that almost every thought I had was false. My thoughts were mostly judgments that happened very quickly. As I mentally saw them as false, it opened my mind to an experience of being inquisitive and watching to see what would happen next. I was delighted to find myself feeling free and happy rather than weighed down with a familiar sense of thinking that I knew everything!

That evening David and I packed our cases ready to leave in the morning. We were full of gratitude for our time with Kathy and Bob and everyone who had come to share the love of Christ with us.

Chapter Thirteen

Power of Decision

Fall 2005

"Being afraid seems to be involuntary; something beyond your own control. ... My control can take over everything that does not matter, while my guidance can direct everything that does, if you so choose. ... The presence of fear shows that you have raised body thoughts to the level of the mind.

The correction of fear is your responsibility. ... You should ask for help in the conditions that have brought the fear about. These conditions always entail a willingness to be separate. ... Before you choose to do anything, ask me if your choice is in accord with mine. If you are sure that it is, there will be no fear." T-2.VI.1-4

Drop It!

The following discussion was with the Holy Spirit as I sat in the car with David, en route to our next destination. I felt slightly grumpy because I'd experienced full-on dreams all night, and I'd not had time for my morning journaling. It seemed like I'd missed out, and I didn't want to read and write in the car.

Journaling

Kirsten: Good morning, Holy Spirit. What can you tell me about my mood?

Holy Spirit: Drop it.

Kirsten: Okay! Anything else? [A smile spread across my face.]

Holy Spirit: Have a wonderful day.

My day was wonderful! It was full of laughter and experiences of oneness. The ego is laughable and should never under any circumstances be taken seriously.

Peace to the World

Journaling

Kirsten: Good Morning, Holy Spirit. What would you have me do or read?

Holy Spirit: Read in the Manual for Teachers, "How is Peace Possible in This World?" M-11

It felt very deep. I had some tears while reading this section, and the following writing flowed from my pen:

> Peace to the world, the Lord has come.
> I remember God.
> I feel His love, His peace, His presence.
> I take Him with me. I bring the Thought of God with me.
> I am the holy child of God, sharing peace and love with my brothers.
> I will turn to the peace of God if ever the thought of death enters my mind.
> Heaven is brought to earth by my remembrance of God.
> The Thought of God is peace.
> I am the Thought of God; therefore, I am peace eternal, and I bring Heaven to earth by my very presence.
> I choose only love.
> I choose only peace.
> I choose to hear God's voice and therefore to bring Heaven to earth.
> Amen.

Carried in the Love of God

David and I drove south to Georgia, where we had a weekend of gatherings at the home of dear friends.

Journaling

Kirsten: Good morning, Holy Spirit. What a wonderful weekend! I felt as if I were floating most of the time. A misty white light embraced everyone and everything, and golden light glowed brightly around the trees framing the gatherings. When speaking I had no awareness of myself as a body. The messages and parables simply flowed through me. The weekend was a beautiful meditation consisting of music, discussions, shared meals, laughter, and silence.

I sank into deep stillness as this writing flowed through my mind and pen:

> I am the child of God. I reflect the Love of God.
> No longer do I believe myself to be a body.
> No longer am I limited. I have been set free.

The End of the World

Today the world ended in my awareness—washed away in the knowledge that the Son of God is innocent. It is that simple. While this realization was coming to me, our host was looking deep into her mind and asking why the world seemed such a painful place to be. As I was writing about how the Son of God is innocent, she realized the only reason for all pain, suffering, and fear was the deep-seated belief in guilt.

I read "How Will the World End?" in the Manual for Teachers. M-14 In deep prayer I realized the truth. A state of profound peace radiated throughout my being as these thoughts and realizations flowed through my mind:

> The Son of God is innocent.
> With this prayer is judgment ended.
> The Son of God is innocent!

With this statement, the awareness that all things
work together for good brings the world to an end.
The world is saved from what I believed it to be.
Right now words cannot describe how I feel. The
world is over. I have fulfilled my function.
My function was forgiveness and the world has
been forgiven.
The Son of God is innocent.
It doesn't matter what seems to play out in the
world now—never again can I be deceived.
All of my experience has brought me to this
moment, to this awareness. I am blessed.

Body Thoughts and the Power of the Mind

Journaling

Kirsten: Good morning, Holy Spirit. I would like another assignment. I'm aware that when I feel pain in my body, my mind
immediately becomes occupied with thinking about how to fix
it. I'd like to focus on the deep teaching from the Course: "The
presence of fear shows that you have raised body thoughts to the
level of the mind." T-2.VI.1 I think this will help me to let go of
the preoccupying "body thoughts" that lead me away from feeling
connected to You. What do you think about this idea?

Holy Spirit: Wonderful!

Kirsten: Is there something I can tell myself, without falling into
denial, each time I experience subtle body aches and limitations?

Holy Spirit: Repeat your goal and bring your awareness to your
changing mind. Say, "I seem to be experiencing body pain, but the
body is not causative, nor is the environment. I am willing to release
this thought entirely."

Kirsten: Thank you. That's perfect! I acknowledge the thought, raise
it up in awareness, and hand it over to you with the willingness to
be wrong about it. This way I stop drawing conclusions about my

body, its limitations, and the effects my actions and circumstances have upon it. Anything else you can tell me?

[A familiar feeling of stiffness in my neck occurs.]

Kirsten: Okay, Holy Spirit, here it is now. My neck is stiff, and when I go to a chiropractor, the pain seems to be released. I want to go to a chiropractor. I give this to You. I can see that I am raising "body thoughts" to the level of mind right now.

I went into prayer and could feel that my perception of what causes body pain ran very, very deep: *I am a body and my neck is stiff and it is affecting me. I cannot be at peace like this.* I could see that I had been holding on to conclusions about what causes body pain and how it could be healed, proving over and over to myself that body thoughts were real.

Kirsten: Wow! So I'm guessing that I will be free of body limitations entirely by practicing this!

Holy Spirit: It's all thought. The body is a thought; pain, aches, muscles, reasons for pain, etc., are all thoughts. The entire world and cosmos consists of layer upon layer of thoughts. By releasing the chain of thoughts, you are freeing the mind to be in the present moment. The body can then be perceived as a temporary holy home for the Son of God and no longer a prison in which you feel trapped. Free your mind; cut the strings. You are not a puppet at the mercy of the body. You are Spirit—Divine Mind.

You have been deciding upon your goal and then setting about achieving it. When you notice that the goal no longer serves you, such as when you are experiencing body pain, you change your goal. You have many goals that are not in alignment with divine mind, and as you bring them to me with the readiness and willingness to release them, you will free yourself of the belief that you are not free.

Kirsten: I feel really excited about this!

Holy Spirit: Wonderful.

Hot Thoughts

David and I drove south towards Florida, where a very excited group of friends had arranged a series of ten gatherings at various Unity churches and Course groups. As we entered the State of Florida, the air conditioning in our car broke. I asked David if we would get it fixed, and he said that it could be expensive, so we would wait to see if an air conditioning shop presented itself in a clear and obvious way. Attack thoughts and feelings of grievance ran through my mind, Why can't we get it fixed immediately? David isn't with me in this. I don't agree with waiting to see if getting it fixed is obvious. I need air conditioning! Why am I in this country? New Zealand is nothing like this. David is tight with money; I would just get it fixed!

I attempted to forgive the thoughts and feelings of discomfort by silently giving them over to the Holy Spirit, but I was struggling with the heat and with deep resistance in my mind. I could feel the intensity of the ego wanting to justify something. As the traffic grew heavier, I could feel that more than wanting to let go of the attack thoughts in my mind about the heat, I wanted David to know that I was very uncomfortable and needed the air conditioning fixed. I made a few comments about how hot it was, how there wasn't any breeze at all, and how I hoped that we could get the AC repaired.

As we continued to sit in the traffic, I fantasized about stopping in a restaurant for a cool drink. It seemed that David and I weren't on the same page. I could feel a sense of separation from him and was afraid to risk suggesting that we stop somewhere in case that was not "guided," and I turned out to be wrong. I didn't know what to do. All I could say was, "It's so hot."

By now sweat was forming a little pool down my shirt, and I had my feet up on the dashboard. In response to my comment about the heat, David looked directly at me with his piercingly bright, blue eyes and said, "Oh, you are having hot thoughts!"

My initial inner response was one of disbelief. Oh, my God! Are you kidding me? Of course I'm having hot thoughts! Who is this man?! How could he not be affected by the sweltering heat? He isn't human! Then it clicked … he wasn't human. The one who was speaking wasn't coming from a human perspective.

Somehow, through my foggy, heat-affected, unhappy state of mind I caught a glimpse of something—a wisp of a distant memory. I could hardly catch hold of it; it was like a thin piece of string blowing in a breeze. I focused my mind with all of the desire I could muster, turning it away from these grievance thoughts and in the direction of receiving help. The thin string transformed into a rope, and I grabbed hold. I looked past the victimization feelings and closed my eyes. I went into prayer, asking to see my underlying beliefs. The following beliefs rose up, and I was willing to be wrong about each of them, in order to have them lifted from my mind.

I believe I am hot because the sun is beating down on the car. I am willing to be wrong about this! [I couldn't imagine what difference it would make to say I was wrong about this because it was so obviously a fact that it was hot!]

I believe I am hot because we are in Florida in a heat wave with no air conditioning. Holy Spirit, I am willing to be wrong about this! I still felt like a non-believer.

I believe I am hot because sweat is dripping from my body.

We are stuck in traffic. I can see the tarmac melting and heat waves rising from the car. [I dropped deeper into how I felt and got in touch with fear.]

I am afraid that the heat is hurting and damaging me. I want to see this differently.

I'm still affected by this world. I get headaches, and I want to protect myself. I want to give this belief to you, Holy Spirit.

I could feel the tension lifting from my mind, and right as I gave over the last thought to the Holy Spirit, a cool breeze floated in through my open window, kissing me on the cheek! I laughed out loud, delighted! "A cool breeze!" I exclaimed, "David, right as I gave over my hot thoughts, a cool breeze came!" David was just as delighted as I was. We beamed with joy, reminded yet again of how loved we are and how everything works together for the highest good. To go through the fire in my mind and pop out the other side of such intensity felt huge for me! It was a miracle! Minutes later the traffic disappeared and we were on the open highway—windows rolled down and the music turned up. We sang along happily and enjoyed the rest of our drive together.

Is This My Life?

When we arrived at our destination, our excited hosts and organizers greeted us warmly. Although I fell in love with everyone I met, I felt concerned, noticing that the average age was about seventy. All of my new friends had white hair and drove slowly. They talked about losing their glasses and running out of time. Thoughts of sacrifice arose: *Oh, my God. Is this my life? Would I ever dance to techno music again? Would I have friends to take long, brisk walks with?* It seemed I had no control over my life. Yes, I was willing to give it all over to the Spirit, and actually I didn't *want* to go out dancing to techno music, but I did feel the intensity of having a split mind. I hid my "unspiritual" thoughts. I found myself secretly praying for people closer to my own age to show up.

I went into prayer and released my age related thoughts to the Spirit. I prayed to be shown that age means nothing and that there truly is no sacrifice. I observed David as he tirelessly met with one group of excited ACIM students after another. I noticed that as the youngest member of the group—sometimes by thirty years—it was me who lagged behind. I was the only one disappearing for afternoon naps!

David lovingly called our friends "elderly beamers," meaning Course students over the age of seventy-five who beam with light and joy! They no longer felt personally responsible for looking after the world and had no interest in working towards future goals or caring about fashion! They were happy!

We stayed in a friend's retirement village where the speed limit was five miles per hour. The residents rode around on large tricycles, taking gifts of food to one another. By the time we left Florida I could happily have stayed there forever!

Floating in Christ

I was coming undone. We were a third of the way through a seven-month trip, and I didn't know if I was going to make it. I had no control over what I wore or ate, where I went, or whether I exercised. I felt like a ball of string that was being unwound. I feared that if I kept unwinding at this pace there would be nothing left of me at all!

Friends had offered us a condominium by the ocean where we could rest for three days between gatherings. One day, going down to the pool,

I was feeling emotional. As David approached me in the water I had a memory of being in the ocean with my brothers. Occasionally, they had playfully dunked me under the water. Feeling vulnerable, I was frightened that David would do the same thing to me. As he moved towards me with arms outstretched, he paused and asked if I was okay. "Are you going to dunk me under?" I asked in a wavery voice. He looked at me with such love and kindness and said, "Oh no, I would never do that." He wrapped his arms around me there in the pool, and I allowed the tears to fall. I felt held in the arms of God.

After the tears subsided, David floated me slowly around the pool for a long time. My world was being retranslated from one of shocks and unexpected surprises to one of tenderness and the utmost care. Each time I experienced a major shift in my perception about myself or the world, I felt the effect within my mind on a deep level. The grip of knowing who I was in relation to the world was loosening.

Chapter Fourteen

Death, Doubts, and a Big Green Monster

Fall 2005

"If you knew Who walks beside you on the way that you have chosen, fear would be impossible." T-18.III.3

Fear of Death

Until we were sitting on the plane, I had not had any fear thoughts about going to Colombia, South America. Out of nowhere I began thinking about being kidnapped and decapitated. I felt awful. I kept turning to the Spirit, but the thoughts continued. As I turned pale David asked me if I was okay. I shared my thoughts of being decapitated, and he held my hand, assuring me that this was not the Spirit's plan. But fear of death continued to arise in my mind, and I prayed and hoped it would go away. Now, because the world out-pictures what is believed, I was also afraid that I might draw the experience to myself, as I have a powerful mind. This awareness added to the pressure of wanting my thoughts to be healed quickly.

A few hours and two flight stops later, we were sitting in the transit lounge in Cartagena awaiting our flight to Cali. Tears were falling down my cheeks as the fear was not subsiding. I felt that I was running out of time. An idea flashed through my mind. I said to the Spirit, "Okay. If I have to experience decapitation or have to see it with my own eyes, can it please be on television because I really don't want this body to have to go through that experience. It feels too extreme."

Turning to David for a hug, I cried for a moment. When I looked up I noticed a small television on the wall in front of me. A movie I'd not seen before was playing in which Kim Basinger was trying to protect a young girl who had supernatural powers. As I watched I couldn't believe my eyes. The young girl was chased into a subway station by a gang of attackers, and as Kim arrived at the station, she found the girl propped up against a wall. As she touched her shoulder gently and asked if she was okay, the girl's head rolled off!

I was shocked! Caught up in the movie, my first response was upset and projection! "How could they be showing this movie in an airport lounge? There are kids here!" I said to David. He looked at me with his big blue eyes and said, "It's all for you, Kirsten." It started to sink in that this movie was my prayer being answered. Taking this flight and stopping in this very airport lounge at this exact time truly was all for me. *Everything* in the world was here to support my awakening. Yet again I was blown away by the Spirit's amazing plan for the healing of my mind!

Oh, thank you, Spirit! Crying tears of gratitude and joy, I gave David a huge hug. It felt so deep and profound. Arriving in Cali, I was enveloped in so much love by our beloved Colombian ACIM friends that any tiny doubts and fears I'd had of being harmed were well and truly washed away.

Comparison and Self-Doubt

We stayed with Lili, a vibrant and attractive young woman living with her serene teenage daughter. Lili lived day-to-day, barely able to cover her living expenses. When her Course group were considering venues for our month of evening gatherings, it was decided that her central city apartment was the most convenient.

Lili was thrilled to host us for the month in Columbia. Being around Lili, a "free spirit" who laughs, loves, and lives with abandon, was stirring up all kinds of feelings within me—from inspiration and delight to comparison and self-doubt. Deep within my heart I desired to be truly free and to live without fear of consequences. Simply being around Lili showed me, by comparison, how limited and controlled my thinking was. David was also inspired by Lili's free-spirited nature. It wasn't long before I sank into deep realms of healing around jealousy and possessiveness.

Lili and the Ring

Lili's mother came to visit us. Noticing David's ring she began asking him about relationships. David told her that his ring was a symbol of union with God. This was true and I sat in agreement. He slipped the ring off his finger and happily waved it around, saying, "A ring has no beginning and no end. It's a symbol of marriage, of union. The ring itself isn't important." He extended the ring to Lili, saying, "I could give it to you." He extended it to Lili's mother, saying "Or to you!" He went on to explain, "It's not a symbol of a marriage to a person. It's a symbol of marriage to God, a symbol of marriage to Divine Love."

It's one thing to talk about a wedding ring being a symbol of marriage to God, but when David offered the ring to the others I felt a contraction in my stomach—it was like a big, dark, empty hole. Fear thoughts sprang up: *How could he say that! I could tell that he meant it!*

And yet we had such a deep commitment; I knew David loved me. My mind was scrambling for safety, trying to convince myself that he wouldn't really give the ring to someone else. *Surely he wouldn't do it without talking it through with me first!* I assured myself that no one would actually take the ring, knowing that David was married to and traveling with me. But beneath these justifying and self-protective thoughts I knew the truth of the matter. David could give the ring away! Joyfully! His commitment to the Spirit's plan of awakening was above and beyond a commitment to anything in this world—including me. He was totally unattached to a ring and to the notion that it somehow bound us together.

I had no choice but to redirect my desire for safety to Jesus.

Losing My Grip

The bottom was dropping out of my world. I'd never been in a relationship where the other person wasn't trying to keep me, wasn't afraid of losing me, wasn't—on some level—trying to reassure me that I was special. Now I was experiencing that not only was I not special, but that everything that was "mine" could be offered to someone else. It struck me down to the core. Down to the core of the "self" who had worked hard, who had put in the effort to achieve something—a position, safety, some kind of security. It all meant nothing to the Spirit. I felt as though my life was being offered to another on a silver platter.

Until I'd come to Colombia, I had no idea that I was attached to David and was invested in my life with him. Now it was glaringly obvious that I was suffering from both.

Feeling the ugliness of competition with Lili, I was unable to welcome her in my heart or support her in loosening from a life she felt trapped in. In this state of mind I was unable to connect with David either. Walking in the streets of Cali, I played "Return to Innocence" by Enigma over and over and allowed the intensity to move through and the tears to fall.

After a while I found myself in a small park where there were people living on park benches, sharing all that they had. My thoughts subsided as I realized I was being shown something. Somehow a crack opened in my mind and the light began to shine through. I saw the defensive thoughts: *Now that I have pulled away, I could protect myself further from David by staying away. I should stay away for hours so that he would know how hurt I am.* But the ego's grip was loosening. The light grew stronger until I felt grateful. Smaller waves of doubt arose, tempting me to maintain a sense of separation. Feeling a strong prompt to return to the apartment, I left the park.

Feeling guilty for pulling away, I walked in the apartment door to a warm invitation from David and Lili to watch *50 First Dates*, which is about having the past wiped away and falling in love for the first time every day.

What If I Am the Ego?

Journaling

Kirsten: Good morning, Holy Spirit. I'm still having many thoughts coming up about being replaced, and possessiveness about my role and relationship with David. Please help.

Holy Spirit: Either your heart is in it or it's not.

Kirsten: Right now it's not. I don't want to be in this relationship. It's too hard.

Holy Spirit: It's all thoughts—thoughts that someone else may travel with David instead of you, thoughts of the future, thoughts of relationships. Give them all to me and trust me. I will guide you.

Kirsten: Okay. I know it's all ego because I'm flipping between feeling safe and vulnerable, between feeling trust and doubt. I am afraid that David will drop me. Surely he will if he discovers that I am the ego! Only the ego can feel jealous and resentful. I am not the presence of Love. I feel so torn right now.

Holy Spirit: What do you want?

Kirsten: The peace of God ... and another life.

Holy Spirit: Herein lies the problem. You cannot have two worlds.

Kirsten: Tell me about my relationship with David.

Holy Spirit: You asked for holy relationship; you prayed for the peace of God; you desired a whole and healed mind. In answer to this, you've been given one who is very advanced and can help you on your way. Your relationship is not of this world. When you compare it or make it different than what it is, the result is conflict and confusion.

Kirsten: [I sigh with relief.] Thank you. And the jealousy?

Holy Spirit: The same. You know in your heart that you share the same purpose—that you cannot own, possess, or limit love. It is only when you try that you end up feeling hurt by your thoughts.

My Life! My Mystic!

Journaling

Kirsten: Good morning, Holy Spirit. Help me! I still feel angry with David for offering everything to Lili. I'm in a marriage involving everyone, but I don't want to feel replaceable. I want to feel special! I feel bad for having these thoughts, for wanting to have everything and feel safe. Is there a reason why I should have more than Lili? Why I should be welcomed and cared for, with food and shelter provided, and she shouldn't? No. It's about possessiveness.

I don't want to feel like this, but I see I want specialness, to know that I am of value. What can you tell me about possessiveness and relationships? About my annoyance at David's loving treatment of her?

[I did not hear a clear teaching from the Spirit in response, but I felt moved to sit in silence for a while. As I sat, a horrible jealousy arose within me. It felt terrible. I finally understood what people meant when they referred the big "green-eyed monster." I almost gagged on the feeling, but I let it intensify and come up like an exorcism. I stayed very still. There was nothing else I could do. Finally it faded and dissolved. The Spirit guided me to read, "Because I will to know myself, I see you as God's Son and my brother." T-9.II.12 Finally, I saw Lili and David as innocent in my mind.]

I love Lili and David with all of my heart. I don't want to feel separate from them. I want the peace of God, to know my brother as myself. Thank you, Holy Spirit. The darkness has been exposed and released. Thank God that's over!

Ownership Is Identity Confusion

Journaling

Kirsten: Good morning, Holy Spirit. The gathering last night was great. I feel very clear and peaceful. What would you have me do or read?

Holy Spirit: Enjoy the peace. Read Review Lesson 52, "I am upset because I see what is not there. I see only the past. My mind is preoccupied with past thoughts. I see nothing as it is now. My thoughts do not mean anything."

Kirsten: I read it through and take many notes. That's a full-on review lesson. Anything to add?

Holy Spirit: Everything you perceive in the world and as thoughts in your mind—including all images and conclusions about the world, people, and your relationships—are the same. They are based on a world that isn't there. They are based on private thoughts, and in perceiving them you feel separate, which is "cause" for upset. Withdraw your faith in illusions. Keep the awareness in mind that this world is made up and has nothing to do with reality.

Kirsten: So my experience of upset over the belief that my life and my security with David was threatened by being offered to someone else—how is that related to this?

Holy Spirit: All that you have is within. All that you have is given by me. The only way that you can lose me is by blocking me from your awareness. Fear does this. You lost the awareness of me yesterday when you were in fear/anger/jealousy. How could someone give your life away? What do you perceive is being given? By whom and to whom? Remember who you are and who your brother is. How can part of your Self give you away to another part of yourself?

In love there is no loss. Love extends to itself. In giving all that you have to your brother, you are giving all that you have to yourself. This is true giving. What would you keep that you would not share with your brother? Would you see him suffer or go without when you have so much to give, knowing that you cannot be without?

Kirsten: Of course not—that's where the guilt comes in. I'm getting this now; this lesson between three people is for the whole world. Ownership and possession is of no value unless it is used for a holy purpose. Or is this still ownership?

Holy Spirit: Give all that you have to me; know that you are one with *all*. Withholding or possessing a part of the whole is the cause of conflict and identity confusion. As you clear this belief from your mind, you will see things differently. You will see all things as equal and neutral, provided by me as symbols and props that are helpful in your awakening. When you believe in ownership, this is what you see—inequality. People, houses, cars, and countries, each belonging to "others." A fragmented world where oneness is impossible.

Kirsten: Thank you so much. This feels deep. I have never felt jealousy or possessiveness in a relationship before, and now I know the full extent of it. The whole world is based on ownership and possession.

Mary Poppins and Midriffs

One night after a gathering we noticed that my clothes were serving as a distraction. The men were trying to work out what kind of a female figure was underneath, and the young women at the gatherings couldn't relate to me.

The "elderly beamers" in Florida loved my "Mary Poppins" look, which consisted of a button-down blouse, shapeless below-the-knee skirt, and sensible shoes. In Cali, Colombia, however—the plastic surgery capital of the world—Mary Poppins was obviously not what was called for!

Exploring this idea with David, it became clear that my clothes were a distraction from the depth of the message that poured through him at the gatherings. David pronounced, "You have to let the Spirit dress you."

Lili, who had the figure of a model and wore mini-skirts, platform shoes and little midriff tops, was delighted at the prospect of taking me shopping! David, who was always up for an adventure, came along too. My mind was split, playing both sides. I was secretly happy at the thought of being seen as "attractive," and yet I felt fear and hatred at the thought of attention being focused on my body. My old "perfectionist" thoughts arose. I wanted to find the perfect outfit that appeared so *casually* attractive that no-one would know I cared. Agh ... the ego! Obviously, I had a lot of pride and body identification to undo.

Lili knew where to take me. She found perfectly fitting clothes in every store we visited. I said yes to long pants and gentle no's to a few small tops. My reaction to one top was, "No! I can't wear this!" Lili curiously asked, "Why not?" I responded, "Because my nipples are showing!" Lili looked bewildered; clearly, she couldn't comprehend why that was a problem.

I tried to explain: "I can't have my nipples showing at a Course gathering." Puzzled, she asked, "What's wrong with your nipples?" David delightedly watched the entire scenario, enjoying Lili's innocent responses to my ideas about inappropriate clothing. As their gentle laughter washed over me, I surrendered and gave my trust over to the Spirit shopping through Lili. She knew what would be perfect for the gatherings. The sooner I let her decide for me, the sooner I would be laughing with them at the ego's thoughts.

Many young women in Cali felt a constant pressure to be physically attractive. This went well beyond simply being attractive to men. Most of the population in Colombia lived on one dollar a day, making the job market highly competitive. It was so extreme that some women were required to have plastic surgery in order to keep their jobs.

The Spirit poured through David and me in such a full and deep way that evening. I felt more deeply rooted in my function than I had in a long time. Lili was absolutely beaming; she had played an essential part in supporting the Spirit's plan for this gathering. I realized how intense things had been for her and the faith required of her to host us and the gatherings at her apartment. I had been so focused on feelings of jealousy and unworthiness in my own mind that I had not been available to support Lili at all.

Once again I was deeply moved by David's awareness of the Christ and how uncompromising he was regarding where and with whom he was meant to be at all times. He was constantly aligned with what served the highest good. This sometimes meant leaving me alone to move through what I needed to see for myself with the Spirit. Incidentally, I loved the clothes Lili had chosen for me. I wore them until they were threadbare!

Search and Destroy

Journaling

Kirsten: Good morning, Holy Spirit. I still have some residual feelings of jealousy. What would you have me do?

Holy Spirit: Read Review Lesson 53, "My meaningless thoughts are showing me a meaningless world. I am upset because I see a meaningless world. A meaningless world engenders fear. God did not create a meaningless world. My thoughts are images I have made."

Kirsten: I read the lesson. Anything else you would tell me?

Holy Spirit: Use your real thoughts for seeing. Do not value an insane and meaningless world where chaos rules, and life seems hopeless and devoid of safety.

Kirsten: I see my insane thoughts are causing my ridiculous feelings, and I know it's the ego because of the drive to prove myself right and condemn David. My mind goes on a search and destroy mission and can't wait to prove him guilty so I can be right and then ... what? Leave? The ego doesn't think that far ahead! I want to see with my real thoughts.

[I drop into silence and a prayer of embracing truth flows from my pen. I write: I trust in reality. I acknowledge that a meaningless world does not exist, and I determine to withdraw trust from it. What I see reflects my thoughts. Loss, suffering, and death are the representation of my thoughts. I let my real thoughts cast their light on what I see. God's way is sure; my images cannot prevail against Him because that is not my will. My will is God's will. I will place no other gods before Him. I abide with God in my perfect home. Thank you, Holy Spirit.]

Do you have an assignment for me today?

Holy Spirit: Read through what you have written.

Kirsten: Thank you, Holy Spirit. I'll be on the lookout for opportunities to apply the truth to my thoughts all day.

Chapter Fifteen
The Grand Finale in Cali

Fall 2005

"Nothing you can do can change Eternal Love." C-5.6

The "Right" Decision

David was invited to Medellin, Colombia for a weekend of gatherings and I felt to stay in Cali. I was invited by four different friends to spend the weekend with them, and I found myself not knowing what to do. I felt the pressure of making the right decision and was concerned that I could get it wrong and miss out on being where the Spirit would have me be. I turned to the Holy Spirit.

Journaling

Kirsten: Good morning, Holy Spirit. What would you have me do?

Holy Spirit: Remember me. You are getting caught up in the world as if it means something, as if the figures in the dream—the things, places, and events—are meaningful in themselves. The world's a stage, and the props are meaningless unless given to me to communicate to you with.

Kirsten: Okay. I give them all back to you, including the belief that I am needed. I will be guided by You. I want only peace.

[I went into prayer and felt at peace. Very soon a phone call came in and I knew I should pack and go with friends to their farm in Papayan for the weekend.]

Weekend with Angels

Journaling

Kirsten: Good morning, Holy Spirit. Talk to me about last night. I know I can't but be in the right place at the right time, but I felt a slight urge to be somewhere else, spending the weekend differently.

Holy Spirit: You could have spent the weekend elsewhere and with different people, but the truth is that who you are with is always the right setting for learning and healing to take place. You can choose to spend your weekend in doubt, wondering if you should be elsewhere, or you can spend every moment with me, devoted to God. Remember that I can use any and all of the symbols/props around you to guide you home but only when your awareness is with me. Doubt is of the ego and it blocks your awareness of me.

Kirsten: So everything is perfect?

Holy Spirit: It is when you spend every moment with me.

Kirsten: Thank you. I feel clear. Anything I should read?

Holy Spirit: Read Lesson 291, "This is a day of stillness and peace." Spend every moment with me, aware of me, as if holding my hand. Remember stillness and peace.

I had a wonderful weekend with my new friends, two of whom had profound mystical experiences and changes in perception. We meditated for hours, listened to angelic music, took siestas, toasted marshmallows, and sang around the campfire.

Back in the Fire

Journaling

Kirsten: Good morning, Holy Spirit. I feel self-conscious. There is so much emphasis on the body here in this city. I feel torn between rejecting all focus on the body and wanting to be attractive. There are beautiful women everywhere, many of whom have had plastic surgery. It's like walking past supermodels every day. In New Zealand I was happy in t-shirts and jeans. At the Peace House I underwent a huge process of letting go of caring about looks, as well as beliefs in nutrition, diet, and exercise. Now I find I'm judging myself and everyone else based on looks. Help! I want out.

Holy Spirit: Give the body thoughts to me. The body is not who you are. It is not your home. It has nothing to do with God's Love for you. All body thoughts are of the ego, regardless of how dressed up they appear to be.

Kirsten: I know, and I can't stand it. I don't like compliments about the body—let alone leering looks from men—any more than I like criticism. I don't want myself or anyone else to focus on it. The constant, thinly disguised focus on the body is why it's hard to be here. The ego gets competitive and wants to look "as good as." I start judging and objectifying myself, and others, and before long I'm in hell.

Holy Spirit: Give it all to me. It's good that it has come up into awareness. It was already in the mind, and now it is coming up to be released. The pressure comes from feeling that you have to act on the thoughts, that you have to look better or different, that you are not perfect and as God created you.

Kirsten: Okay, Holy Spirit. I give all of these body thoughts to you. I don't want to repress, reject, or act on any of them. I want to know myself as whole. I want to know my brothers and sisters as God created them to be. Is there anything else? I still feel tired and tearful. I don't want to be here. I don't want to be around people.

I want to be with David and to rest. I don't want to think about anyone else, problems, or the future.

Holy Spirit: Give all of your worries to me.

Look to the Spirit for Love and Understanding

Maria and I met at the gatherings in Colombia. We felt an instant connection with each other. Maria was a devoted Course student, and she felt that the Spirit had brought me to Colombia just for her! Her husband had passed away some years before. I was invited to stay at her quiet, two-bedroom apartment which was only five minutes from Lili's place. The contrast between the two environments was like night and day. Lili's place was high energy, with horns blaring constantly in the streets below. Lili herself was also highly energetic and spontaneous. One or the other of us was often going through some kind of emotional crisis. This invitation from Maria was the Spirit offering me a quiet respite. Sensing my hesitation, David said he would visit me at Maria's and that I could return to Lili's place anytime I felt the need to do so.

Taking a small bag with me to Maria's house, I found myself sinking into stillness immediately. It had been a while since I'd felt so relaxed. That evening I felt I needed to have a quiet night, rather than go to the gathering. I asked David if he would come to be with me after the gathering. He said no, that he would stay at Lili's apartment. I expressed my need for him to come back, and he said that he needed rest and would be up in the early morning hours to answer emails. Maria's apartment was only five minutes away, and, with email access at both houses, his answer didn't make any sense to me. I felt very alone and upset. *I thought we were supposed to be in this together, that David would be here for me if I needed him.* Waking the next morning, I still felt anguish that I was apart from David.

Journaling

Kirsten: Good morning, Holy Spirit. Please help me. I'm still holding onto the feeling that David should have stayed with me.

Holy Spirit: Read Workbook Lesson 293, "All fear is past and only love is here."

I read and took notes: All fear is past and only love is here. Let go of past mistakes. See only present love, a forgiven world. Let go of everything that is unlike love.

Holy Spirit: Let it go. Trust in me. There is always a different way of seeing. Give past mistakes and your perceptions of your brother's mistakes to me. Let them go and ask to see with me. Forgive your brother.

Kirsten: I want to let this go. I'm still holding onto hurt and anger, and I want only peace. I give it all to you.

Holy Spirit: Well done, my child. Now you can hear my voice. Remember, I am always with you; you are never alone. Every experience is for the purpose of healing. Rely not on form for your safety and peace, or you will be hurt and disappointed. Last night you were in the perfect place with one who loves you. It is only your lack of trust that can disturb your peace. All things work together for good. Trust in me always. You have called on healing, and healing is what you are going through. Trust this always. This is what you want. Let the fear come up, and look to me for love and understanding, not to your own thoughts of how it should be.

Kirsten: Oh, that's it. It's my own version of how it should be that is always the problem. It comes with a feeling of injustice and leads to distressing feelings, which are all based on hypotheticals. Whew. Thank you so much.

Holy Spirit: I love you.

Desire for Joining

Journaling

Kirsten: Good morning, Holy Spirit. What message do you have for me today?

Holy Spirit: This is all for you. Every moment of this day is for you. The script was written long ago, and you can observe from a place of safety. Pay attention to the messages you receive today. There are no accidents; I am with you. Turn to me for clarity and right perception if you are in doubt at any time.

Kirsten: Last night David told me of a conversation he'd had with our friend Carlos, who had noticed that although there were many

Course groups in Cali, they seemed to be separate. Carlos wished they would join together. This morning it was mentioned that three Course groups were coming together for the first time to join us at the gathering! No accidents!

Holy Spirit: Perfect. Never underestimate the power of the mind that joins with the desire for healing.

Kirsten: I can feel it. Anything to add?

Holy Spirit: Read Workbook Lesson 36, "My holiness envelops everything I see."

[I read through the lesson and had a wonderful day.]

The Past Resurfaces

In a few days, David and I would catch our return flight back to Florida, where we'd left our car, before continuing on our journey to the South Pacific. The time in Cali had been a full-on month in which I faced the fear of death, jealousy, possessiveness, and body thoughts—all the while surrounded by the continual buzz of car alarms, mobile phones, and the general go-go-go of a big city. To top it all off, I received an email from Simon, my past love.

We hadn't been in communication for two years, but he'd certainly come to my mind when I had entertained thoughts of escaping to the past. The timing of Simon's email was unbelievable—it came right when I had been going through such intensity and was at a decision point. My relationship with Simon had been light and exploratory, whereas my relationship with David involved facing the darkest of the dark in my mind. It seemed insane to consciously choose this for myself!

And who could I even share my doubts with? *No one* would encourage me to stay in a relationship that was all about relinquishing independence and facing every type of darkness imaginable. No one would understand except for David. However, when I was doubting my relationship with him my mind wanted to turn elsewhere.

Journaling

Kirsten: Good morning, Holy Spirit. I feel so sad. I want to be with Simon. I feel trapped, and I don't want to be here. I don't want to move forward with any plans, but I can't go backwards either. Miami is a disaster zone—tornadoes have ripped through the area, and our car that we left there may be totally wrecked. This feels like a reflection of my mind. Fleeing to New Zealand won't help since it's even further away from Simon, who is in England. What if he and I are supposed to reunite? Now that I know about the ego, and that this was what we were facing when we were together, I think that we could heal anything that came up!

Initially it felt good to be in touch with Simon, and I replied to his first email, pouring out the amazing experience of my life over the past two years. But when he wrote again a lot of sadness came up for me.

I knew I had to talk with David, even though I was afraid to share my thoughts and feelings about Simon. I felt disloyal and thought that surely David would tell me to leave. But his response was the total opposite of what the ego had said it would be. David was utterly loving and supportive—he was the epitome of unconditional love. He reminded me that our relationship was for healing and that it was all voluntary. I couldn't believe it when he said, "Would you like to look at flights to England and go and visit Simon?" He joined me fully in the exploration, as if it were no different than any other healing moment. I couldn't believe how generous he was. He wasn't trying to keep me or to control anything. In fact he was willing to help me leave with such loving kindness that I couldn't hold back the tears. I felt safe and innocent and able to explore my thoughts fully with the Spirit. It felt like the softest thing in the world.

Together, David and I explored the idea of looking for flights. As we opened up an airline website, I remembered what it was *actually* like to be with Simon. Although it had been a loving and helpful relationship at a time when I was beginning to explore spirituality, it had been well and truly maxed out. Simon's path was not one of mysticism, and mine was. I had already tried to hold onto the relationship way past it's completion date.

With the spacious support being extended by David, I could intuitively feel that flying to London was not the direction I was to take. It didn't feel expansive; in fact, it felt small and fraught with "what if's."

This experience with David was an even deeper insight into the purpose of holy relationship. The context of the relationship was to provide a place in which to stay together with the Spirit, no matter what was arising to be looked at. Within this context, I was innocent—no matter what came up for healing. My trust in David and his devotion to purpose deepened again that day. He truly wanted what was best for my awakening. I felt it in every part of my soul.

Releasing the Past to Know Love

Journaling

Kirsten: Good morning, Holy Spirit. I am beginning to feel a gentle peace regarding Simon. He sent a long email with a link to his website with photos on it. Seeing how happy he is with his life warms my heart and confirms that our lives have gone in different directions. I don't want to resist, reject, or project anymore. I want only to trust You.

Holy Spirit: Stay with me. Read Workbook Lesson 345, "I offer only miracles today for I would have them be returned to me." Read also, "Principles of Miracles," Numbers 23-25 from the Text.

I read the sections and took these notes: Hide nothing and you are willing to enter into communion and understand peace and joy. Use time constructively. Miracles are part of an interlocking chain of forgiveness, which when completed is the Atonement.

Kirsten: I am here only to be truly helpful. [I stand up to leave and feel almost pushed back down onto the couch. We were obviously not finished! I suddenly remembered that over the recent months my mind had been preoccupied with past thoughts about my family and Simon, that clearly hadn't been released.] Anything else, Holy Spirit?

Holy Spirit: You are the extension of love. You are the extension of all that is. Give without expectation of any kind and you will know God. Give without the thought of return in the future and you will know God. To know God is to be like Him. God gives all without conditions. Your relationships with all of your brothers, including Simon and your family members, are no exception to this practice. You are projecting the past onto them.

Unless you release the past entirely, you do not desire to know them truly. Love does not involve the past and you know by the busy imaginings of your mind when a relationship is unholy and not of pure Love. Simon is an opportunity to forgive and heal. Love does not have levels or special targets, and it does not lead into the future with a sense of stress or urgency.

Kirsten: I feel peaceful and content now. My heart is filled with gratitude.

Later I realized that there was no one else with whom I could share this depth of healing with because there was no one else that I was *supposed* to be sharing it with at this time! David was the one given by the Spirit. In opening up and including David, I had dared to face the guilt and fear that it was wrong to even have these thoughts and feelings, which invited him to hold my hand and walk with me through it. In the end there was nothing to do and no new steps to take. The healing occurred within my mind. It was an allowance of my desire for the "safety" of the past and the world as I had known it to be fully released from my mind.

Mystical Moments

The three organizers who had invited us to Colombia were excited to take us to the Juan Valdez National Coffee Park. We had a day free of gathering and it was the perfect weather for a day trip. The park was a beautiful botanical garden with gentle pathways, sitting areas, and little cafes. As we approached one of the cafes, I began to go into a mystical experience.

My perception changed, and everything went very soft and hazy. The gardens glowed; it was much like being in the ocean and seeing everything contained within the water. Everything was connected. I couldn't understand what anyone said. The voices sounded as if they were coming from above the water, whereas I had dropped deep beneath the surface where everything was One and Known. David noticed my sudden state of child-like wonder. Knowing intuitively what was happening, he took my hand.

I couldn't read the menu or speak. David ordered me a coffee and an ice cream for himself, which felt perfect! Everything felt perfect. I was happily silent and apparently looked as if I were about five years old. After we left the coffee shop, David held my hand as we slowly walked through the gardens, following behind everyone else.

The only moment I experienced fear was when one of our friends looked at me and seemed to be asking a question and expecting a response.

I couldn't understand a word she said, but David answered for me. For a couple of hours I floated happily through the gardens, holding David's hand as our friends chirped away like happy birds. Everyone was laughing and pointing at various flowers and gardens. So beautiful.

Is the Course for Everyone?

We had our final gathering in Colombia two days later, at a Course student's farm. She and her group were very excited about the Course. They were in the early passionate phase of wanting to tell the whole world about it and bring everyone along.

Our host brought up the subject of her employee, a man in his late sixties who had lived his entire life on the farm. He interacted with people on the property, and once a month he took a brief trip into town for supplies. She asked David if she should invite him into their Course group. David asked her to describe his state of mind. She shared the fact that he was always happy and grateful, thanking God when it rained and when the sun shone. He deeply appreciated every aspect of his work and loved living on the farm.

Our host was worried that if her employee wasn't aware that it was all an illusion then he might not wake up. She thought that perhaps she should bring him into the group so that he could learn the metaphysics. "No!" was the resounding chorus from David and several of our friends who'd spent the last three weeks with us—one of whom joyfully exclaimed, "Keep the book away from him!"

Our host was quite surprised. David went on to speak about the curriculum of forgiveness being for everyone, but the Course itself being one path among many. *A Course in Miracles* came as an answer to a prayer from two highly educated research psychologists who were dissatisfied with their work and calling for a deeper connection with God. They were calling to be unwound from an intellectually driven life, which was on the opposite end of the spectrum to this man's simple life of prayer, gratitude, and awareness of divine providence.

How beautiful and relaxing it was to think of this smiling man as a symbol of one who was on his path, rather than as one in need of education.

Chapter Sixteen

Don't Let Go

Fall 2005

"Learn, then, the happy habit of response to all temptation to perceive yourself as weak and miserable with these words: I am as God created me. His Son can suffer nothing. And I am His Son." T-31.VIII.5

Off to Venezuela

Leaving our beloved friends in Colombia, we headed for Venezuela where Carolina and her Course group would host us for two weeks. The Spirit guided me to go back to basics and repeat some of the early Workbook Lessons. When I believed the world was in chaos around me and my emotions were high, the early lessons were perfect for focusing my thoughts and applying the teachings. It was the same as the first time I did the lessons—I found that no matter what was happening, my lesson for the day was the perfect answer to every situation.

The president of Venezuela was enacting mock war games against the U.S. during our visit. To me it was a perfect reflection of the volatility going on in my own mind! Other Course teachers had been invited to the country to teach during the "games" but had refused because of the "high-risk factor." As always, David went where the Spirit guided. His encounters were always miraculous in nature, whether they were with people holding babies or people holding machine guns. This trip was clearly part of a larger plan of awakening for me. There was absolutely no question of whether we should be there or not.

Our hosts had poured their hearts into promoting our visit in order to cover our airfares and reach all manner of groups. Carolina had set up television and radio interviews with David to let everyone in the region know about our upcoming gatherings. She believed that everyone wanted to awaken and that everyone should know about the gift that was on its way!

I joined in on two of the radio interviews and saw how the Spirit could speak to any topic. The show hosts felt heard and supported by David's words and became as engaged as any sincere Course student. On the sports show—in between the announcer reading the soccer scores—David spoke on the importance of mind training, team collaboration, and the power and glory of being "in the zone." He even went so far as to introduce the idea that sports injuries were related to guilt in the mind. On the "Looking for Love" show, he spoke about holy relationship and finding divine love within our own hearts. The famous Venezuelan romance radio host was in total agreement that this was what everyone truly desires!

The Venezuelans were just as excited to be with David as the Colombians had been. David had happily adapted to the South American 10 p.m. dinner schedules, and he fully embraced their 11 p.m. espresso coffee parties, staying up late to make the most of every opportunity to be together and answer questions.

Trust and Freedom

"The only way to heal is to be healed. The miracle extends without your help, but you are needed that it can begin. Accept the miracle of healing, and it will go forth because of what it is." T-27.V.1

Journaling

Kirsten: Good morning, Holy Spirit. Yesterday on the TV show I was happy to find I wasn't feeling nervous. But the presenter asked me a question about war. Would there have been a better reply? How can I tune in to let you speak through me more clearly so that I don't doubt myself?

Holy Spirit: It was perfect. You don't know what kind of effect your reply has had on others, and I can assure you that what was said was perfect. Trust in divine order. When you doubt, you block your awareness of me—even doubting after an event blocks your awareness. Every moment is an opportunity to ask me for guidance. Trust that all things work together for good.

Kirsten: Today I'm on Workbook Lesson 10, "My thoughts do not mean anything." What else can you tell me about it?

Holy Spirit: Your thoughts show you a world. What you perceive comes from your thoughts. When you purify your mind by clearing it of judgment, you will see a forgiven world, a peaceful world, a gentle world born anew in every moment. You are looking upon a world based on your preconceived ideas of the past. You are making assumptions and drawing conclusions from what you see, based on the past. To empty your mind is to release the world from what you think it is. This is freedom. Freedom comes from your state of mind. To forgive is to release yourself from the past. The past is simply ideas in the mind, all of which come from your perceptions.

Kirsten: How does this fit with feeling like I'm experiencing something for the first time?

Holy Spirit: Let's look at the concept of "for the first time." The first thought that involved perceptual experience was within time. Eternity does not involve time. The Spirit does not have perceptual experiences within time. The ego is the belief in time and space. Bring your awareness to the present moment, the closest point to eternity that you can come to while believing in time and space, and every experience will seem new.

Kirsten: I'm thinking back to my teaching experiences, for example, teaching a child to read. Is this a case of the ego teaching ego concepts to itself?

Holy Spirit: Every moment is an opportunity to experience present love, joining, and joy. Teaching a child to read is a backdrop for joining. Ego concepts such as reading and writing can be used by the Spirit. Your role is to remember who you are and who your brother is in truth. Practice forgiveness, and turn to me for guidance when needed. There is nothing new about the world of form. It is a world of images that can be used to free your mind; that is its purpose. Seen from this perspective, every moment is a new opportunity.

What If This Is as Good as It Gets?

Our first gathering in Merida was on the topic of holy relationship. There were around two hundred people present. I was starting to feel maxed out. Being on stage in front of an audience was too much for me. There was nowhere for the ego to hide, and I certainly couldn't fake being healed or enthusiastic when it wasn't my genuine experience.

The following night we had a movie gathering to watch the movie, *As Good As It Gets*. David gave a talk to set the movie up. After it was over I joined David on the stage for the post-movie discussion.

In the movie, Helen Hunt had cried out that her life and her relationship were not her choice. This line had affected me deeply, but it wasn't until I was on the stage that I felt the full effect of it. I felt undone by that line! And there I was in the spotlight, unable to move or make a sound.

We went for a meal with our organizers after the gathering and I felt completely disconnected. I couldn't answer any of the questions about how hungry we were or what we wanted to eat. I noticed David giving me a questioning look. I felt separate from him and was afraid to speak the thoughts and feelings that I couldn't understand. I interpreted the thoughts to mean that everything was wrong, that my life with him wasn't my path after all. I was afraid David would confirm this if I shared it with him. I kept it to myself that night.

Frozen

Journaling

Kirsten: Good morning, Holy Spirit. Last night on the stage I felt awful—cold and shaky, emotionally stirred up, and blocked. I wanted to get down and sit at the back of the room, but I felt paralyzed. I kept asking you for help, but it all felt so disjointed that I couldn't hear your voice. What can you tell me?

Holy Spirit: The ego was stirred up. To look back on a scene with regret or fear, wishing it were different, is to perceive through the ego's lens. All things work together for good. Remember, there are no exceptions except in the ego's judgment.

Kirsten: I'm considering the lessons learned from the experience, but I realize now that I'm perceiving them as lessons for the next time so that I don't have to go through that experience again. But this is still the ego. The lessons learned are already past, over and done. They have nothing to do with an imaginary future. What can you tell me about this?

Holy Spirit: You have picked up on this subtle ego trick several times. Trying to protect the future, no matter how disguised it may appear as helpfulness, is the ego. Right now you can choose to focus on the guilty past or on a hypothetical future, both of which are nowhere but in your imagination, keeping you distracted from the present moment. Or you can give your fears and doubts to me. Remember, there is only one mind; there is no one outside of you judging you. You are doing it all to yourself, and you can let it go now.

Kirsten: Okay. I give all of my thoughts to you. I want only peace and to know myself as perfect. When I apply my lesson, "I am upset because I see a meaningless world," to all of this, I am amazed at how it is the perfect answer. W-12 Doing this to myself is upsetting and makes my whole world meaningless! Thank you!

Be Gentle

Although I was feeling grateful for the clarity, I still had some residual fear, so I shared my experience from the movie night with David. He lovingly reminded me of the context of awakening. I was going through a disillusionment, a deep transformation of consciousness within which these thoughts and feelings were completely normal. He reminded me that I was answering a very deep call to awaken and that I had full permission to step back at any time to rest. I felt so much better upon hearing this.

When in fear, my default mode was to push myself to be "supportive and helpful" rather than to listen inwardly. It was clear in retrospect that I was afraid of going up on the stage, and now I realized that I need not have taken that action at all. There truly were no expectations of me.

David kept reminding me that it was all for me and that I was completely loved no matter what I did or didn't do. This was very hard for me to accept; clearly, I had to keep being reminded of the truth. I had to learn to trust in my own devotion, beyond being "the best Course student" or "the best traveling companion" I could be. Of course I would show up, and of course I would be of full availability and service whenever I could, it truly was my joy. But if the guidance was to step back and rest, I had to learn to honor that too. Pushing myself did not result in miracles!

Wrongness and Undoing

"The way out of conflict between two opposing thought systems is clearly to choose one and relinquish the other. If you identify with your thought system, and you cannot escape this, and if you accept two thought systems which are in complete disagreement, peace of mind is impossible. If you teach both, which you will surely do as long as you accept both, you are teaching conflict and learning it. Yet you do want peace, or you would not have called upon the Voice for peace to help you. Its lesson is not insane; the conflict is." T-6.V.B.5

I was acutely aware of the two thought systems within my mind: the fear-based thought system of the ego and the love-based thought system of the Holy Spirit. When I was not in my right mind, the ego felt as if it was being stretched and pushed simply from being around David—who was a constant and uncompromising reminder of the light.

Our seven-month trip was so packed full that there was nowhere for the ego to hide. When resistance was high, ego thoughts would arise in my mind: *I'm not David. David has found his calling; he is a talking mystic. But I'm not! I have nothing of value to say.* Catching these thoughts helped me to spot the ego trick that sees differences and personality types as real identities, and then it uses the perception of differences as a defense against surrendering to oneness.

Over and over again I saw that my self-concept or "small self" can never know its own best interests because it is this very self that is being undone. It is made up of memories, feelings, and behaviors which it defends and justifies as being right, and being "me!" Thank God I always remembered to call upon Jesus' often quoted question from the Course: "Do you prefer that you be right or happy?", which helped me recognize that I was unhappy and self-righteous. T-29.VII.1

Like a light dawning in my mind, I would remember that I had made a choice. It was a choice to blame David for how I was feeling and to insist that something was wrong. This choice resulted in making him untrustworthy in my eyes, and without trust I had nothing—no peace of mind, no love, no light, no purpose, no joy, and no David as my mighty companion.

I knew that I had to stay very close to David in my mind. The slightest siding with the ego left room for a shadow to come between us and was a sure detour into darkness and pain. With no gap, I was with him in total trust in God, and everything fell back into divine order.

Another Plan

Carolina, our Venezuelan host's journey with *A Course in Miracles* was an experiential approach. She combined her love of music, improvised dance, and theatre with her Course study and inner inquiry. It was an intimate healing process with the Spirit, which developed into what she called IntroDanza—inner dance. As the years had progressed, her lessons with the Spirit had become classes which she taught to groups of students. I joined in with several of her classes and found them to be very gentle for my mind. I loved music and movement, and I embraced it all as a welcome gift from the Spirit.

My year in the alpine village of Wanaka felt akin to Carolina's experience with IntroDanza—the development of a gentle and spacious inner listening. It was a time when my heart was opening and when I was being shown how to "follow the music" and let the Spirit lead the way. However, since traveling with David, even though he was a consistently loving presence, my path had felt steep and the pace felt very fast. Because I was with someone whose mind was already unplugged from the ways of the world, I was constantly made aware of where my thinking was still hooked into the ego.

I was going through a deep dismantling and letting go of specialness, and part of my mind was saying, *no, I don't want to give up me*. I didn't have the stamina to keep up with David's tireless energy. We were like salmon swimming upstream, where there were many points of having to leap forward and upwards to continue on. David was leaping and jumping in joy, and I was swimming as fast as I could just trying to keep up with him.

Observing the contrast between David's tireless availability and energy and me being on the edge of exhaustion, Carolina shared a parable with me from her childhood. Her ten-year-old cousin ran up to her four-year-old cousin one day, excitedly grabbing her hand. He began running, saying, "Come and see! I want to show you something!" He was so excited that he didn't notice his little sister had fallen and was being dragged across gravel. Her little knees were bleeding. Carolina likened the ten-year-old to David and the four-year-old to me, which felt accurate to me in that moment.

At times I could've curled up in her arms and said, "Yes, it's too hard!" Her life certainly seemed easier, her path gentler and slower. Being shown the Course lessons through music, movement, and dance within my own bedroom with candles burning? Oh, that felt so welcome!

Carolina invited me to join her in a partnership to open an IntroDanza school with her in Venezuela. It felt like an opportunity to be the teacher rather than the student. With David, I was always the student because I was the one going through intense changes and being shown what was in need of correction, whereas he was always happy.

Over the past months various friends had said, "You're just like David," and, "You're a female David." Of course, the presence of the Spirit shining through David and me was the same, but only I knew how active the ego was in my mind at other times.

There was still so much to be undone! I had beliefs about who I was, how to be healthy, and how to be a good friend, partner, listener, and lover. And what better way than to partner me up with one who was not impressed or affected by any of it? I was nowhere near the same as David in terms of being in a consistently peaceful state of mind, and it took a constant willingness to be honest and humble in order to stay open to the help I needed.

When I was very honest with myself, I knew that I was meant to stay with David. I was in the midst of a deep undoing process that I wanted to continue with. I felt like a caterpillar in a chrysalis—hanging upside down in the dark, going through a metamorphosis that I had no control over. All I could do was allow the process and trust that at some point I would emerge into the sunshine, light and free.

David and I talked about Carolina's invitation to stay and open a school with her. As always, David was very receptive and open-minded to new ideas. Exploring the possibilities together, David said that I didn't have to leave to dive into something new. He suggested that I invite Carolina to America, where I could travel with her and host IntroDanza gatherings. This was the perfect solution.

Integrity

I stayed in Merida to rest and continue with some internet projects while David went to another city to hold gatherings. The subject of integrity had been raised at gatherings over the past two weeks, so I asked the Spirit about it.

Journaling

Kirsten: Good morning, Holy Spirit. I feel resistance to getting on with my internet tasks. Tell me about this feeling of not wanting to start.

Holy Spirit: What matters is your state of mind. When integrity is in question, your whole world is in question. The tiniest doubt in your mind is guilt, and guilt blocks me from your awareness. This is why integrity is so important. Not for reasons of getting tasks done, but for the healing of your mind. You have undertaken a mind training process that is bringing you to a consistently peaceful state of mind. Every time you invite doubt through your lack of integrity, you are stalling the process.

[I meditate on this for a while and remember recent conversations where I had entertained the possibility that my path could look different to how it is now. David wasn't present during those conversations and right before he left for his weekend away, I felt a little foggy and distant from him.]

Kirsten: What else can you tell me about integrity?

Holy Spirit: Integrity is honesty. To say what you mean and mean what you say is to have integrity with yourself, and therefore with everyone. Lack of integrity is dishonesty. I will always guide you to do what is most helpful for all concerned. To refuse, forget, or reject my guidance is clearly a lack of integrity.

Whose guidance are you following if you are not following mine? When you align your mind with me, you devote your mind to God, to love, to healing, and to peace. Every time you experience doubt, it is because of your own lack of integrity. It is this simple. The remedy is also very simple. Stop and ask me what I would have you do. Ask yourself if you are being honest about your motivation. Is your desire single or split?

When you are aligned with me, your thoughts come from me. Your actions are then guided by our thought—and motivation is pure. When motivation is of God, you feel safe, certain, and able to watch the script play out. When your motivation comes from a split desire, there is a sense of personal responsibility, urgency, and stress, and these feelings are often pushed out of awareness. Whenever you sense the slightest feeling of secrecy, you can be sure the ego is involved. Turn to me. Recognize that your desire is split, and ask yourself if your motivation is of God.

Kirsten: Thank you Holy Spirit.

Only Love Is Real

Journaling

Kirsten: Good morning, Holy Spirit. What can you tell me about my Workbook Lesson today, "I am not alone in experiencing the effects of my thoughts." W-19

Holy Spirit: All minds are joined.

Kirsten: How can they seem to be thinking differently?

Holy Spirit: All thoughts are either true or false. Thoughts are either from me, and are of God, or they are about nothing, and are of fear. When the mind releases the ego, all thoughts will be as one. All understanding will radiate and flow throughout the mind. All thoughts will be loving. The mind asleep, believing itself to be separate individual minds thinking their own thoughts, seems to be thinking apart from God. When you believe yourself to be a private mind, you believe everyone thinks differently. This is what you project, and this is what you perceive.

Kirsten: What about Jesus? What did he perceive?

Holy Spirit: He resurrected his mind. He released the belief in the ego, which is the belief that you can be separate and think apart from God. His eyes still perceived different bodies, and he heard words spoken by those who believed they were separate from God, but he knew the false was false. He was able to heal because he knew that only love is real, nothing else. With this knowledge, the love, strength, and power of God radiates through the open channel of the mind, healing and blessing simply by being Itself. All doubt, fear, and death disappear when the light has come.

Kirsten: It seems so simple.

Holy Spirit: It is!

Kirsten: Only love is real. I will remember this thought today and always.

Chapter Seventeen
Imprisonment versus Freedom

Fall 2005

"The Holy Spirit teaches you the difference between pain and joy. That is the same as saying He teaches you the difference between imprisonment and freedom. You cannot make this distinction without Him because you have taught yourself that imprisonment is freedom." T-8.II.5

"You still have too much faith in the body as a source of strength. What plans do you make that do not involve its comfort or protection or enjoyment in some way?" T-18.VII.1

"A holy relationship is a means of saving time. One instant spent together with your brother restores the universe to both of you. You are prepared. Now you need but to remember you need do nothing. It would be far more profitable now merely to concentrate on this than to consider what you should do." T-18.VII.5

Keep Your Hand in Mine

David and I were preparing to leave Venezuela and go to Florida for a rest period before flying to New Zealand. I had contacted friends in the North Island who were happy to arrange gatherings with us. Part of our mission in New Zealand was to fly to Wanaka in the South Island to collect my car and the rest of my belongings.

Journaling

Kirsten: Good morning, Holy Spirit. I booked the tickets for us to fly down to the South Island. Immediately after sending a suggested itinerary to the organizers, I had doubts about everything. I had a strong impulse to cancel this trip and our gatherings. Help!

Holy Spirit: When your motivation involves covering costs, such as plane tickets, you put yourself under pressure to perform. The spiritual journey is about healing your own mind, nothing else. Remember your one goal. Give your fears and doubts to me. Trust that the plans will be given you as they were this morning. Remember that your only responsibility is to accept the healing for yourself. David is joined with you—loving you, supporting you, holding your hand whenever you need help. It is you who withdraws your hand and then feels alone.

Keep your hand in David's, as his is in mine. Remember your promise to do God's Will, not your own. Trust that you will receive each perfect step in your awakening plan, one moment at a time. Let the fears and doubts come up for release, and remember it is my hand you are holding.

Kirsten: I don't want to do gatherings right now. Why did I set them up in New Zealand? Am I setting myself up to fail? I feel mixed up.

Holy Spirit: You don't have to do any gatherings right now. I set up the gatherings in New Zealand. They are part of the plan. Those who want healing will step up, and the gatherings will unfold perfectly. You are not responsible. It is only the ego's judgment that makes things seem difficult. Return to peace now. All is perfect. You are loved.

What Do I Really Want?

Journaling

Kirsten: Good morning, Holy Spirit. Can you talk to me about the best use of time, living a devotional life, and purpose? I also have questions about following my heart and feeling free. I judge myself when I'm not focused. I want to relax and enjoy life without guilt.

Holy Spirit: Yes. It is important to be clear about the best use of time. There is no difference between these three phrases; best use of time, devotional life, and purpose; they all mean the same thing. They are helpful phrases for mind-watching and keeping your mind in alignment with mine. Devoting your life to the highest purpose there is—healing your mind, and waking up to the remembrance of God—is a decision that you make and apply your mind to in every moment.

Your actions are the demonstration of your decision. It is never the other way around. This is why I have told you many times that the Course is highly individualized; it does not have to look a certain way. I will always direct your use of time in a way that joins you with your brothers and with God. This takes many forms including meditation, prayer, and communication.

The ego's use of time involves avoidance, immediate gratification, and reinforcing separation through "doing it my way." You are wise to these tricks and are devoted to not acting when you are in doubt as to which voice you are hearing. Feeling free and following your heart are both states of mind and are identical in their expression. Following your heart is following my guidance. I am your heart in the sense that your deepest desire is to remember God, and I am your communication with God. I am your guide to love.

The ego's idea of freedom is to have many choices, and its version of follow your heart is to try to choose the best illusion out of the many. You know by the way that you feel when you are choosing amongst images. There's a feeling of, "I hope I choose the right one; I hope I don't make a mistake." When listening to the ego, following your heart is likely to involve going off alone. Separation is always a factor in the ego's plan.

Kirsten: This is so helpful. Right now the ego keeps coming in with so many options for the future. Immediately I sense the choose-your-favorite-image game, which I cannot play. I know it's a game. I've done the manifesting thing; I created my life the way I wanted it to be many times, and now I want only to listen to you. But part of my mind still wants to experience things in this lifetime.

This feels confusing because these things are future-oriented. Can I still move in a direction I feel would be a beautiful experience? Is this still trying to manipulate the script?

Holy Spirit: The script is written. At certain times in your life you believed you were in control and directing the play. This was a state of mind. You can feel this way now if you choose to. You have control over your state of mind, how you perceive the world, and whether to listen to and follow my guidance or not.

As you continue to trust, to open up and relax, to sink into your mind and be the observer, you will watch the same script play out from a place of peace. Rather than feeling that you are directing the play and are therefore responsible for how it plays out, you can enjoy watching from a place of safety, trusting that all things work together for good, and letting all things be exactly as they are.

Trust. The plans will be given you. You will be told what to do, where to go, whom to speak to, which tickets to purchase, which plans to change. All things work together for good. There are no exceptions. I am with you. Trust.

Kirsten: I sometimes ask myself whether I'm following my heart. When David asks me, "What do you want?" I can't reply with anything in form. I can't reply with a place or an image. I have intuitive feelings about possibilities for the future, but they are not here right now except in my mind as ideas. Is there any difference between ideas in my mind and what seems to happen in form? Are they all equally unreal?

Holy Spirit: Yes. All are images. All are possibilities. However, they can be helpful stepping stones for guiding you home. The Love of God can shine through all of them. Intuitive feelings of peace, love, and happiness come from me. Relax. When the time comes for the next step in your plan, it will be given you. There is no need for effort on your part. There is no need to try to work out the script, to plan for the future, to worry about anything at all. Trust in me.

Turning Right-Side Up

David and I had round trip tickets to New Zealand, but I began to consider not returning to the U.S. with him in March. The past months had been intense, and the idea of being based at *A Course in Miracles* healing center with Jackie in New Zealand, felt like a slower paced option. I discovered that I could refund part of my airfare if I chose to stay in New Zealand, and I began to seriously contemplate this as a possibility.

However, rather than ease my mind, the fact that I could change my ticket tormented me. I felt pressured about needing to know the future so that I wouldn't waste money.

We had a ten-day rest period planned at our dear friend Frannie's house in Florida before taking the long journey to New Zealand. I was experiencing a lot of doubt and confusion about my direction and my purpose, and right at that time David received an invitation to visit with friends in Europe. He kindly invited me to go with him, but I wasn't in any state to go on another big trip.

I looked forward to having my own room in a quiet house, in a quiet neighborhood. Frannie was retired, and was delighted to have me stay, and rest. She deeply appreciated the Course, and the work we were doing, and she loved having the opportunity to provide a peaceful haven for David and I, in the midst of our travels. She was an angel. No doubt about it.

Journaling

Kirsten: Good morning, Holy Spirit. Talk to me about the last two sentences of Workbook Lesson 20, "I am determined to see. What you desire you will see. Such is the real law of cause and effect as it operates in the world." W-20.5

Holy Spirit: What you desire you will see. This is the reversal of the thinking of the world. What you see actually comes from what you think. What you think comes from your desire. Desire God, peace, and miracles, and your vision is in alignment with my vision. This lesson is a step in helping you realize that you do not see with the vision of Christ and you want to see differently. It allows your mind to be turned right-side up.

Kirsten: Is it really true? That I see what I desire, that everything I see comes from my thoughts? I experience this often but not always. It seems like the screen of the world is there. I choose to see it and to write my interpretation on it. Like going to a new city—Merida in Venezuela, for example—and seeing the mountains and the surroundings. I believe they were all there before I arrived.

Holy Spirit: Every moment is new when your focus is in the present moment. As I've explained before, Jesus heard and saw differences, but he put them all in the same category—false.

The sleeping mind projects thoughts as images onto the screen and forgets immediately that it has done so in order to then experience the effects of the projection as real. When you believe yourself to be a body or a figure on the screen, it seems real. All of the myriad of concepts seem real; memories of past experiences seem real; interpretations based on past experiences seem real. From this removed state of thinking, the mind believes itself to be in the world and separate from God.

Kirsten: It's so clear. What else can I do to keep remembering the truth? When we use the word *screen* I think of a two-dimensional screen, like a television. But looking up and seeing a ceiling, for example, makes all of this seem so real. It's hard to imagine it being a screen.

Holy Spirit: There's no need to try to figure out illusions. You cannot solve an impossible situation, especially while you still believe in it. Continue to ask me for guidance, and continue to follow my guidance, including about how to use and apply the Course every day.

Fear of Loss

I felt fear arising, so I went to talk to David about how I felt. Now that he was going to Europe without me, I was afraid I was making decisions that would result in separation. The fear felt deep. Although I'd had many thoughts about wanting to escape to the past—to go back to New Zealand—I had not acted on them. I had always turned my attention towards forgiveness.

But as soon as I initiated the idea of not returning to the U.S. with David in March, he was invited to travel to Europe without me.

David told me that sin is the belief that you've done something wrong, and guilt is the emotion that arises from sin. All fear is fear of punishment. The thought "It's not my fault," is a defense against the feared punishment. He said there are only two emotions—love and fear—and that all emotions that are not loving, are derivatives of fear. They seem different, but they really aren't.

David walked out of the room, leaving me feeling scattered, my mind in turmoil. I meditated for a while, focusing on letting it all go and trying to remember that I didn't need anything from anyone. The source of my worry was a sense of need. I tried to remind myself that I had everything I needed right now.

When David came back into the room, I shared the insight that my fear was coming from a belief in lack. He said, "Whatever you perceive is lacking from a situation is what you have failed to give." Somehow this helped me to reverse the direction of my thinking, and peace returned at last. My lesson for the day just happened to be Workbook Lesson 21, "I am determined to see things differently." Very helpful!

Personal Goals Are Ego Goals

Journaling

Kirsten: Good morning, Holy Spirit. I have been reading Workbook Lesson 25, "I do not know what anything is for." I feel I know the difference between ego, or personal goals, and your goals. Your goals involve joining and healing the mind. They are communications of love and blessing. I can feel the understanding of real purpose each time I apply the lesson to things, thoughts, and situations; for example, "I do not know what this laptop is for."

Holy Spirit: Wonderful.

Kirsten: This lesson feels like a good reminder to look at the purpose I give to my actions.

Holy Spirit: The statement "I do not know what anything is for" will hold you in a state of humility. Humility is a state in which you are open to receive. The "I know mind" is the height of ego arrogance. My role is to guide you home to the remembrance of God, which is a process of releasing the world from what you made it for. To hold onto beliefs of "knowledge" of any kind about this world is to hold onto a lie. The world is false. Real knowledge has nothing whatsoever to do with this world; it is beyond this world.

Kirsten: So what does it mean when I say *I know* the difference between ego purpose and your purpose?

Holy Spirit: This is discernment. You are using the word "know" as a verb, as a helpful step in the direction of knowledge. You could also say, "I *can tell* the difference between ego purpose and holy purpose." With regard to the mind, you are unlearning; you are training your mind to release ego beliefs. This process does not involve acquiring knowledge. When I use the term "knowledge," I am referring to experience in the truest sense of the word. God can be but known. God cannot be learned. The path to God is one of forgiveness, of humility, of accepting the truth about your Self. It is a surrender, a yielding. The kingdom of Heaven is within.

Making Decisions without Guilt

I asked the Spirit for explicit guidance as to whether I should stay in New Zealand after March, or return to the U.S. with David. The following day, Frannie invited me to go with her to a psychic. As soon as we met, the psychic offered me a reading.

She told me very clearly that I had projects to get on with in New Zealand and that David and I would have more than one base. She felt that I would be based in New Zealand for the following year, and David would continue to accept invitations to travel. She told me that David and I were soul mates and best friends and that we shared a strong purpose.

I took my meeting with her as confirmation that I was to stay in New Zealand instead of returning to the U.S. with David. Initially, the decision came with a sense of peace, but before long fears and doubts came up.

Journaling

Kirsten: Good morning, Holy Spirit. I felt a huge sense of relief after the reading with the psychic yesterday, but now I feel like I made a wrong decision. Why do I feel so anxious and personally responsible?

Holy Spirit: Guilt. Guilt is in the mind, and you are projecting guilt out onto the screen and then making decisions to avoid it. Hence the confusion.

Kirsten: Yes. Then I fear having made a wrong decision based on trying to avoid making a wrong decision. And then I want to reverse it. This is insanity. It's all because I want to avoid guilt. Is there something I should do?

Immediately the "I Need Do Nothing" section from the Course came to mind, and I relaxed. "A holy relationship is a means of saving time. One instant spent together with your brother restores the universe to both of you. You are prepared. Now you need but to remember you need do nothing. It would be far more profitable now merely to concentrate on this than to consider what you should do." T-18.VII.5

Why do my decisions always feel so big? Like I'm changing the course of my destiny?

Holy Spirit: Decisions feel big when they involve the intense emotions of separation, guilt, and fear. The first seeming decision made "alone" was a trial separation from God. Any decision that reflects this idea, no matter how subtle, reminds the ego of what it thinks it has done. It then wants to avoid the feeling.

You asked, "Should I do something?" Yes. Give your fears, your doubts, and your thoughts involving guilt to me. Listen to my guidance and trust that all things work together for good. The ego wants to act to change things on the screen. But when the cause of the problem is guilt, how can tinkering around with form solve it?

The problem is at the level of mind. Release the guilt and you will find there is no problem to solve.

[I cry with gratitude and relief. I go through all of the thoughts in my mind, releasing them to the Holy Spirit.]

Holy Spirit: What do you want?

Kirsten: A place like the house where I was staying in New Zealand, with a supportive community. A home base with plenty of space to meditate, have Course meetings, do Inner Dance, watch movies, and have gatherings. I want to be in constant communication with you.

Holy Spirit: I am always with you.

Kirsten: Sometimes I can't hear you.

Holy Spirit: Do you hear my Voice now?

Kirsten: Yes. Is there something specific that I can read if I find myself in that state of confusion again?

Holy Spirit: "I who am host to God am worthy of Him. He Who established His dwelling place in me created it as He would have it be. It is not needful that I make it ready for Him, but only that I do not interfere with His plan to restore to me my own awareness of my readiness, which is eternal. I need add nothing to His plan. But to receive it, I must be willing not to substitute my own in place of it." T-18.IV.5

The Justice of Heaven

When David returned from Europe I picked him up at the Miami airport. We stopped on the way back to Frannie's house to talk about everything that had been unfolding for me. I shared all of my thoughts and feelings about New Zealand, as well as what the psychic had told me.

We had a deep discussion about how anxiety and doubt come from vacillating on the commitment to purpose, and I became willing once more to let go of all my ideas about the future. I wanted only to be guided by the Spirit.

When David woke up the following morning he told me he'd had an epiphany about New Zealand, and that my staying on was part of the Spirit's Plan. It was a clear sign to me that nothing had gone wrong. I felt so happy!

Journaling

Kirsten: Good morning, Holy Spirit. I feel wonderful. After talking it all through with David, I know that everything is going according to plan. David will return to the U.S. in March, and I will stay in New Zealand. He may come back the following summer; either way, we won't be apart for too long. There is no separation. We are joined in purpose. [I cry tears of relief and gratitude.] I am so relieved. I love David so much, and I don't ever want to separate from him. Do you have anything to tell me about this?

Holy Spirit: Trust saw you through. You shared all of your thoughts and feelings with the willingness to listen and follow whatever the plan may be in form. And with this willingness comes Heaven. All that your Father wants for you is your happiness. [I cry more tears of relief, gratitude, and happiness.] Sweet child, do not doubt your Father's love.

Of course you will be given your heart's desire. But when you do not *know* your heart's desire, how can it be given you? Would you recognize your highest good when a veil of fear cloaks your awareness of it? Do not be afraid to express your heart's desire. Even if it is spoken of in terms of form, this is but a symbol of your desire to live a life of love and happiness, extending your Father's Love to your brothers. Your inspiration will inspire others. Your passion will ignite passion in others. Shine your light, my child, and let it be seen by all. You have a beautiful gift to share. Do not be afraid to hold it up and offer it to all who would join with you.

I was guided to read, "The Justice of Heaven" and laughed out loud at how perfect this section was in regards to my experience of the past twenty-four hours. In it Jesus says, "What can it be but arrogance to think your little errors cannot be undone by Heaven's justice?" T-25.IX.1

Chapter Eighteen
Two Worlds Collide

Winter 2005

When you are aligned with Me
your thoughts come from Me.
Your actions are then guided by Our thoughts,
and motivation is pure.
When Our motivation is of God you feel safe, certain,
and able to watch the script play out.

Do not doubt your brother,
he is the Son of God.
Hear, seek and trust My voice in him.
Love, accept, and appreciate your brother
to know your Self as whole.

You and your brother are One

Letting Go of Specifics

Winter had arrived in the U.S. and David was delighted that we were heading down to the South Pacific for another summer. He loved the idea of traveling light and moving with the seasons. We farewelled Frannie in Florida and took our first flight on the long journey towards New Zealand. Our first stop was the transit lounge in the airport in Chicago. The ego was stirred up within me and seemed to be intensifying with every step we took towards my 'home country.' I felt as if there was a growing divide between myself and David. It took everything I had to keep turning back towards him and welcoming him as a Presence of Love and not as the cause of my inner conflict and stress. I was facing the core problem of trying to maintain "two worlds." I felt tormented.

Since I couldn't reconcile the two worlds, it made me want to push either David or everyone in New Zealand away. Trying to bring the two worlds together—that is, having David meet everyone from my past—felt like combining oil and water. I knew they wouldn't mix and that I would be caught in the middle, having to choose, having to sacrifice either being with him or being with the others. No matter how I tried to resolve it within my mind, I couldn't find a meeting point. I felt very stressed.

These thoughts came up with such intensity and so quickly that I could barely catch them. I didn't want to admit or speak them aloud because they arose with guilt and a feeling of disloyalty. But if I didn't expose them to David, I found myself blaming him for making me feel this way.

I shared these thoughts and fears with David and, as always, he was an angel of support, giving a full and clear context for what I was facing. But the thoughts and fears continued to arise again and again. I could tell that underneath it all I must not yet have made the full decision to let it all go. I turned to the Holy Spirit in prayer:

Journaling

Kirsten: Holy Spirit, I have repetitive worry thoughts about going to New Zealand and staying there next year. When it's just me and David, I can bring my doubt thoughts to you for healing. I'm afraid of being in New Zealand where there are people who know me well and may pick up that I have doubts about David and this path. It is intense enough already without having witnesses to my doubts.

I'm supposed to be a way-shower, a demonstration. I want people to know that David is trustworthy. But right now I feel like a complete fake about everything. What if someone asks me if I'm happily married to David? I can't say I'm happily married! How can I possibly reply? I don't have to define or explain myself at the Peace House or with mighty companions, but my mind is going crazy with feeling that I have to prove something to those from my past. Right now, I just want to hide. Oh my God, it already feels so intense.

Holy Spirit: What do you want?

Kirsten: Peace. To feel in purpose. To have no fear.

Holy Spirit: In this moment, is there anything to fear?

Kirsten: No, nothing. Fear is laughable right now; I can see that my thoughts are all future projections. But I feel pressured by the feeling that I could do something wrong now that will affect the future.

Holy Spirit: How about if you knew you could not mess it up, that you are loved no matter what?

Kirsten: [I feel blessed relief.]

Holy Spirit: Relax with this. Enjoy today.

Choices

"The issue of authority is really a question of authorship. When you have an authority problem, it is always because you believe you are the author of yourself and project your delusion onto others. You then perceive the situation as one in which others are literally fighting you for your authorship. This is the fundamental error of all those who believe they have usurped the power of God. This belief is very frightening to them, but hardly troubles God. He is, however, eager to undo it, not to punish His children, but only because He knows that it makes them unhappy." T-3.VI.8

Journaling

Kirsten: Good morning, Holy Spirit. Anything to tell me?

Holy Spirit: Yes. As you know, if what you want comes from ego desire, you are choosing nothing, and this road will lead you to disappointment and unhappiness. When what you want is God and your desire is single, the form will unfold, reflecting your desire.

Kirsten: Through talking with David I've uncovered that I am afraid of love, and that I have an authority problem. It's a relief to uncover this. I want peace and guidance from you. Every time I decide upon the form, I lose the feeling of my purpose. It is so clear that worrying about how things will work out in form is where the fear comes in. I'm still worried that my decision to stay on in New Zealand was influenced by my preferences.

Holy Spirit: You have the power to correct this mistake right now. Simply release the desire to be right about it. Release the fear. I will guide you. It will be obvious. Trust me.

Kirsten: Why can't you be more specific about whether I should refund part of a return ticket to New Zealand or not?

Holy Spirit: Specifics are of the ego. I am concerned only with your state of mind—your happiness—right now. Binding yourself to specifics blocks your awareness of present joy.

No Stones or Obstacles

David and I stopped in San Francisco overnight on the way to New Zealand.

Journaling

Kirsten: Good morning, Holy Spirit. Will David and I take our wedding rings off? David has talked about how the symbol of us traveling together as husband and wife is serving Spirit's purpose now, and yet it is obvious that a change in form is coming.

Holy Spirit: ... silence ...

Kirsten: [I feel a deep sense of peace.] I feel close and easy with David now. I recognize that autonomy was at the core of my fear around bringing my two worlds together. After making the decision to fully commit to this path and my purpose again, the projection onto David stopped. Finally, I feel I can relax and trust that being in New Zealand will be fine.

Holy Spirit: Good. It's all a reflection of your mind. As you become clear about your purpose, and your commitment, and as your readiness to go deeper increases, you will continue to "discover" ease. The "problems" will continue to melt away before you. This is the meaning of, "He will go before you making straight your path, and leaving in your way no stones to trip on, and no obstacles to bar your way." T-20.IV.8 The stones and obstacles are of your making. As you step forward, willing to trust God and let go of your fears, the obstacles disappear.

Kirsten: David and I have talked about opening a branch of the Foundation for the Awakening Mind in New Zealand. I feel unable to predict the future. I feel present and peaceful with this. I want to watch the unfolding. Is this resistance? I recognize that I have some preferences.

Holy Spirit: You are perfect. You are loved. You are a blessing to everyone you are with and to everyone who has been touched by your presence. Things will unfold perfectly and you will be told and guided, one step at a time. Preferences, when held onto as idols, represent fear of God and therefore death. Preferences, including loved ones, when given to me with willingness and trust, represent opportunities to extend God's Love, to experience joy and much laughter.

Embrace your life. Embrace everyone in your life without fear or concern about preferences. Your willingness to release special relationships and embrace holy relationship is a beautiful demonstration for the whole world. Inclusion is the nature of God's Love.

Following the "Big Yes"

We flew from San Francisco to Auckland, and arrived to a loving welcome from Jackie and Roger at the airport. They drove us north to the Hibiscus Coast, where we would be based at their family home for the next two and a half months.

Journaling

Kirsten: Good morning, Holy Spirit. I have a concern about money. Will the gatherings in New Zealand bring in enough money to support everything?

Holy Spirit: Give your money concerns to me.

Kirsten: Okay. *I release all of the thoughts in my mind.* Talk to me about InnerDance.

Holy Spirit: Follow your joy. As with all ideas involving form, you must lead with the purpose. Enjoy the process. You know by your happiness and joy that you are following the "Big Yes" in your heart, and this is all that is required as far as organizing and arranging is concerned.

Extending your joy is your purpose, and this in itself guarantees success. It is only when you lead with the form—for example, trying to arrange the form to cover expenses—that you lose sight of your purpose, which is only to extend. By extending love and sharing your living experience, healing occurs and all blocks are shone away. It is this simple.

Shine your light, share your passion and your joy, light up the world. I will arrange the form. "You may think that an enormous amount of time is necessary between readiness and mastery, but let me remind you that time and space are under my control." T-2.VII.7 "When you perform a miracle, I will arrange both time and space to adjust to it." T-2.V.A.1 All you need do is follow your heart, which is listening to my guidance. All else will be added unto you. There will be no obstacles to bar your way because you are not trying to arrange the form to meet illusory fear-based needs.

The path is clear—simply keep your hand in mine and rejoice with me.

I Am the Dreamer of the Dream

Journaling

Kirsten: Good morning, Holy Spirit. I have just read "Reversing Cause and Effect" in the text. This line is so powerful: "The body is released because the mind acknowledges 'this is not done to me, but I am doing this'. And thus the mind is free to make another choice instead." T-28.II.12 It makes it so clear why I must take total responsibility for everything that happens in my life, why I must keep coming back to realizing that I am the dreamer of the dream. The alternative is littleness, which is sickness.

Holy Spirit: Yes. This is reversing cause and effect to their proper perspective.

Kirsten: Any tips for keeping this in mind?

Holy Spirit: Yes. When you start your day, choose the type of day that you would like—for example, a happy, peaceful day. Bring your focus back to this instant. Do not trick yourself into believing that there are things that you *must* do, and that you are then at the mercy of these doings, not knowing how they will play out. This is like reducing the power of the Christ Mind down to a helpless pawn in a game of chess being played on the top of a windy cliff. *You are the dreamer of the dream.* Never forget this. What do you want?

Kirsten: A flowing, happy, peaceful day in which all arrangements and travel plans are confirmed and finished with. One in which I can enjoy a walk on the beach, and visit my brother, his girlfriend, and their new baby if it all fits in easily.

From the text: "The world is full of miracles. They are the dream's alternative, the choice to be the dreamer, rather than deny the active role in making up the dream."

I then had a wonderful day. I kept reminding myself that I am the dreamer of the dream, and all of the things I felt I had wanted to do flowed beautifully.

Letting Go of the Riverbank

David and I would soon travel down to Wanaka to pick up my car and belongings. I had a lot of resistance to letting go of a place that represented freedom in my mind, and I was projecting this resistance onto David.

Journaling

Kirsten: Good morning, Holy Spirit. I am feeling resistance to David. Part of me does not want to be a mystic. Part of me does not want to drop the world right now. I am still tempted to move back to Wanaka and go dancing. Jesus says only a handful of people will go all the way with the Course. Maybe I'm not one of them. I don't want to do it David's way. I want to live in Wanaka. What can you tell me?

Holy Spirit: When resistance is high, hold your hand out and ask for help. You will receive it.

Kirsten: It's fine for David. He is fully supported, he has his part to play and fulfills it perfectly. He is so happy all of the time! Now I know why people get so upset with him. I don't want to speak in front of groups of people anymore; it's not my role. I feel like I'm not enough, like I have to be more, learn more, do more. Please help!

Holy Spirit: Trust and follow through with what has been set in motion. Do not fear the current. Let yourself be taken down the river. The temptation is to stop and go back, but I assure you that down the river is where you want to go.

Kirsten: Should I leave some belongings in Wanaka? Will I go back there?

Holy Spirit: To free your mind of "elsewhere," you must let go of the concept of "going back to Wanaka." This is what is meant by "let go of the bank." You cannot enjoy being taken down the river when you are holding onto long reeds. Remember your last experience in Wanaka.

Kirsten: [I went into prayer and remembered how an old pattern of pushing myself had arisen, and a second sports accident, this time involving skiing, had resulted in concussion. I remembered that I had felt devastated, and fell to my knees, crying out for help. Soon after that, Jesus appeared to me, announcing that he would be my guide. Within two weeks, he had guided me to leave Wanaka. I was lonely during my last month in Wanaka—my purpose for being there had come to an end. Although I had wanted to stay, I knew in my heart that I was to move on in order to deepen in my spiritual journey.]

Holy Spirit: It is time Kirsten. Free your mind. Let go of Wanaka. Trust in divine order.

Kirsten: [I have an image of myself hanging on to a few very long reeds as I am taken down the river and around the corner, trying not to go any further!] What if things don't work out?

Holy Spirit: It is all for you. How could it not work out when you are listening to your heart and following your joy? It's all about your joy. Nothing else. No one else.

Kirsten: Okay. Thank you.

Presents versus Presence

This morning I told David that I wanted to buy presents for my family, since they all had birthdays around Christmas time. I felt guilt around this desire because I knew that the funds we had were all to be used for the Spirit's purposes. David suggested I read the section in The Manual for Teachers on Generosity.

Journaling

Kirsten: Good morning, Holy Spirit. I understand the Generosity section, which says, in essence, that the teacher of God gives away in order to keep, is generous out of Self-interest, does not want anything he cannot give away, and by giving away the things that are of God, they are protected forever for him. But I still feel angry that I can't just buy a present to show my love. I actually feel like I want to keep a secret from David and go and buy one for my nephew without telling him! I need help! Talk to me about generosity.

Holy Spirit: Generosity in the world's terms involves time and ownership. When time is not available as a means for demonstrating generosity, it is often substituted by giving material possessions. Generosity in my terms involves being who you are and reflecting this truth through your actions. In true generosity there is no idolatry, comparisons, financial or time considerations. The teacher of God reflects the giving, generous nature of His father, Who gives unconditionally to all of His sons whether they seem to be aware of His gifts or not. There is no guilt involved when you give as your Father gives. There are only blessings.

Your desire to give is beautiful. Share this desire openly with me, with David, and with those that you love. Ask me if there is a way to express your desire in form and let me guide you.

Kirsten: Okay. Thank you.

After admitting that there were things I wanted to hide from David, the desire to buy presents lessened considerably. What was coming up was deeper than just wanting to buy presents. I recognized a familiar feeling of wanting to have things my way. This was the authority problem that David had discussed with me in Florida. I went into prayer and saw that it was a "two worlds" moment. The ego was projecting onto David that he was stopping me from being able to love my family—sneaky!

I aligned my mind with David and the Spirit, trusting completely that the gift I had to give was my love. No one expected any other gifts, and they kept telling me that my being there was the greatest gift of all. And then I remembered that my older brother had already paved the way for me; he had refused to buy Christmas and birthday presents for years! That made it even easier to see it was the ego that had been insisting I prove my love in such a superficial way. Oh, I still have such a long way to go!

Is It Safe to Let Go?

Journaling

Kirsten: Good morning, Holy Spirit. I want to step back from the role of teaching at gatherings, and I want to stay in one place. I feel lighter now that I am clear about this. The past year has been almost continuous traveling, over thousands and thousands of miles, and all that I have gone through has been shared publicly. It has been intense. Can I retreat now?

Holy Spirit: You can retreat now.

Kirsten: David has talked about his hermitage experiences—having periods of rest, taking bike rides and long walks—and this seems impossible. I can't imagine having rest time like that together. I feel caught in a wheel of having to be productive, do gatherings, and cover costs and air fares. This doesn't fit with doing nothing.

Holy Spirit: Let the fear and anger come up.

Kirsten: How? I feel confused. David has talked to me about it all. Often, after trips overseas, there aren't any funds coming in to help with the costs of operating the ministry in the U.S. So giving everything away for free only works with financial support.

Holy Spirit: What you need will be provided. Release your concerns of "how." I am the "how." I will guide you as to where to be, and I will guide you to be in places and situations where you are supported. You are supported right now.

Kirsten: Yes, but that's only now. What about when David leaves? I can't believe I'm asking this!

Holy Spirit: David is not leaving. Everything in this world is temporary. The use of symbols is temporary, but Love is eternal. You asked for a relationship in which you could experience a love that would never end. This is that experience. You asked for no separation. This is that experience. You asked for the peace of God, and beneath the surface of changing emotions and changing feelings is the peace of God.

Kirsten: [I take a deep breath and the feeling of peace envelops me.]

Chapter Nineteen
Releasing Specialness

Winter/Spring 2005-2006

"Pursuit of specialness is always at the cost of peace. Who can attack his savior and cut him down, yet recognize his strong support? ... You have a function in salvation. Its pursuit will bring you joy. But the pursuit of specialness must bring you pain. Here is a goal that would defeat salvation, and thus run counter to the Will of God." T-24.II.2

"You have come far along the way of truth; too far to falter now. Just one step more, and every vestige of the fear of God will melt away in love." T-24.II.9

Between a Rock and a Hard Place

Although David and I were being hosted by Jackie and Roger, we found ourselves spending considerable time with our ACIM friend, Mia, and her partner, Kevin. Most evenings we enjoyed watching a deep movie with them. Mia and Kevin became inspired to host us. They were exploring the idea of setting up a base for a branch of our ministry in the South Pacific.

David told me he felt guided to stay with them, and I felt split. I was drawn to be with David at Mia and Kevin's because of the singular purpose that we shared, but I didn't want to abandon my family. I felt that Roger would be upset if I chose to stay with others on a full-time basis.

The feeling of being split was acute. No matter who I was with, I felt guilty and wrong, and those feelings were projected onto either my family—namely Roger—or David. I wished Roger would stop trying to hold on to me and instead support me on my spiritual journey. On the surface he was very generous, offering us financial support and a place to stay. But there were veiled attack thoughts and an obvious lack of trust that seeped through into his communications, and I felt it was a personal attack. I was doing all that I could to be true to my spiritual path, and I resented that Roger couldn't fully trust and support me.

When the cause of my hurt and guilt was projected onto David, distressing questions arose. *Why is he making me feel guilty? Why do I have to choose? Am I not allowed to be with my family?* It wasn't at all surprising that David was guided to stay at Mia and Kevin's!

One day I was preparing to drive over to Mia and Kevin's, where David was now staying. Roger said his usual parting words, which triggered guilt in me, "Oh, are you leaving? Why are you going to be with *those* people? Why don't you want to stay here with your family?"

I felt on the verge of collapse. The guilt had become intense, but up until this point I had tried to be "spiritual" and hide it. I couldn't do it any longer. Finally, I allowed myself to be honest about my feelings with him. I said, "When I'm with you and the family, I feel guilty that I'm not with David. When I'm with David, I feel guilty that I'm not with family. In this moment I feel that my heart is telling me to go and be with David, Mia, and Kevin. The only reason I would consider not going is guilt. Guilt over doing the wrong thing by you and causing you pain." Tears welled up, and I felt both sadness that I could hurt him and gratitude for finally being able to share my struggle with him.

He was immediately supportive, saying, "Oh my God, I don't want you to feel guilty! I only want you to be here when you know in your heart that you're *meant* to be here. You never have anything to feel guilty about. I love you so much." It was a distinct moment of healing, of "undoing specialness" by being transparent.

By honestly expressing my true feelings, I had given Roger the opportunity to express what was in his heart as well. It was profound to see that the guilt was truly all in my own mind. By projecting it onto Roger and David, I had maintained it and been caught in what felt like a game of abandonment, where there were no winners. Roger waved me off down the driveway, and I felt a huge relief. The softness of tears was so much better than the tension and anxiety of unexpressed guilt!

Once at Mia's, I shared what was in my heart with everyone. I told them, "I feel like I'm abandoning my family. I feel so guilty when I'm here with you, which keeps me distracted and prevents me from feeling fully present. I need help to know what the Spirit's guidance is."

Something within my mind softened in my daring to be transparent. Rather than feeling alone and wanting to get things right in terms of where I was meant to be, I'd invited everyone to enter in and support me. I hadn't realized how alone I'd felt. Now I felt the undoing of specialness was not just for me to tackle! Everyone could join me in my prayer for healing.

I allowed myself the space to practice listening and following and to learn which voice I was listening to. I discovered that the voice that was telling me to be good and do the right thing was not always the Spirit. By giving myself permission to listen, I developed a clearer sense of when I was following the Spirit as opposed to when I was attempting to minimize guilt.

I learned quickly that the only time I could be with my family was when I was in a miraculous state of mind. In that state, I was able to be present and patient and remain unaffected by family dynamics. I wasn't getting caught in past ways of being and resenting them for it afterwards. Instead, I found them cute!

I was able to join with my family in a lightness that hadn't been possible when I was struggling with guilt. Even an occasional comment such as, "You're not the same as you used to be," would now have me responding in a light and loving way, "No! You don't annoy me anymore! I've taken full responsibility for my state of mind! Aren't you glad?!" I was above the battlefield! Hallelujah!

In this way I was reinforcing innocence—mine and everyone else's—and I would leave my family feeling stable, regardless of what had been spoken or whether there had been uncomfortable moments. I could handle it all because I wasn't making any decisions alone. I knew that everything was for my healing.

If sadness or the belief in abandonment arose in my awareness, it happened when I was with David, which gave me a stable context in which to look at my feelings. There was no avoidance, blame, or projection—or if there was, it didn't last long. Now I was with David one-hundred percent and was no longer blaming him for the intensity I was going through. I wasn't pulling myself away from him, depriving myself of the support I needed.

I was sure that the Spirit would finally get fed up with my ongoing struggles regarding specialness and say, "Enough! You should be healed from this by now." I was yet to learn that the Spirit's plan was a gentle loosening from attachment and an unwinding of the mind, rather than rejection.

No matter how much I wanted this phase of healing to be over with as quickly as possible, it wasn't something that could be rushed. Every day was deeply devoted to prayer, watching my thoughts, and allowing the healing. In facing my fear of separation and choosing to follow the Spirit's plan in each moment, it began to be healed. I started to understand that I was not causing separation from love.

Heading in the Right Direction

David and I flew south to Wanaka to pick up my car and drive it back up to the North Island. I was feeling resistance to the trip and somewhat distant from David. I feared he wouldn't see Wanaka the way I did and that he'd point out that it wasn't special. Wanaka felt like a part of me, and I didn't want to hear that it was an illusion.

I turned to the Course for help, and was guided to read "The Real Alternative" section from Chapter 31:

"... to achieve a goal you must proceed in its direction, not away from it." T-31.IV.7

"All choices in the world depend on this; you choose between your brother and yourself, and you will gain as much as he will lose, and what you lose is what is given him." T-31.IV.8

"Forgive yourself your madness and forget all senseless journeys and all goal-less aims. They have no meaning." T-31.IV.11

Journaling

Kirsten: Good morning, Holy Spirit. I'm very grateful for that reading. God has not left His Thoughts. I forgot His Presence and His Love. There is a choice that I have the power to make. When I search for happiness, a memory of God in the world, it's a futile search. Thank you for the reminder. I feel like I really lost it for a while. What would you have me do now? Where would you have me go?

Holy Spirit: Relax into this. Trust this. Follow what is obviously being provided for you. This path is to God. The experience will continue to be one of healing, joy, and joining.

Kirsten: Talk to me about purpose.

Holy Spirit: The purpose of the world is death. It seems to be a place offering choices and pathways leading to truth and happiness, but the very fact that one desires a pathway in the world—expecting the mystery of life to be unveiled and problems to be solved—is a sure sign that a road to nowhere is about to be embarked upon. The path to God is the recognition that you have it all right now and nothing in form need change for the truth to be known. Your purpose here is to accept the truth and demonstrate your acceptance by joining with your brothers.

Every time you choose to "do" something, expecting an outcome in form, you are choosing illusions, and you have forgotten the basic laws of real cause and effect. Going "somewhere else" to try to achieve a state of mind is like a goldfish swimming from one side of its bowl to the other, expecting to find the ocean. Choose purpose by choosing for God, and allow the form to be what it is—reflections of thoughts.

Kirsten: Thank you.

Releasing Wanaka

As our plane touched down in Wanaka I watched my mind closely to see if it still felt like home to me. I noticed that I didn't have the mystical feeling and emotional swirl in my heart that I'd had previously. As I'd anticipated, David didn't appear impressed by the scenery, and I intuitively felt to keep my mind very focused and not get lost in thinking about and sharing stories of my past experiences there. I was also watching closely to see if there was a strong call for me to be there.

It turned out that most of my friends had moved on, and the few who still lived in the area were away the week we were in town. David and I held a small Course gathering, but those who came were clearly on a different path. Although they enjoyed the gathering, we didn't get the sense that they wanted to explore the Course further.

We picked up my car and began the five-hour drive northwest to stay with our friend Bill in his newly renovated "house bus." Driving away from Wanaka, I once again began to feel torn. Although I'd let Wanaka go many times within my mind, I hadn't released all of my attachment to it and it still represented a place of refuge to me.

After we arrived at Bill's, he offered to let us stay with him for as long as we needed to. Later on I shared my doubt thoughts with David. Night after night I shared my dilemma with David, trying to find the answer as to whether or not I should go back to Wanaka, but it just wasn't resolving. We had gatherings planned in the North Island, and one night, after I had expressed the same doubts again, David said he was going to leave.

He booked a ticket to fly back up to Auckland. I couldn't believe it! "You're leaving me here?" I asked him, feeling completely abandoned. "We have gatherings in the North Island, and I am guided to go now," he replied. David was, yet again, giving me the opportunity to choose. There was literally nothing else he could do in terms of support; I had to come to the decision by myself. The next morning, Bill took David to the airport. I went into prayer and tried to feel my way to making a choice: north to Auckland, or southeast to Wanaka? But I couldn't feel anything.

Bill had been up north for the summer. The following day he was going to continue his journey south. He invited me to follow him in my car and stay with him until I knew which direction to go. Not knowing what else to do, I followed Bill south. The first two hours felt like driving into a void. I continued to pray. The further south we went, the more I began to notice something ... Aha! I could feel it! South was not the direction I was supposed to go! I continued to follow Bill, exploring the feeling and asking the Spirit to make it clear. As if passing from under a dark storm cloud, the awareness of guidance began to shine in my mind again. I remembered! The direction had always been to collect my car and leave Wanaka.

Tears began to fall as I realized that Wanaka was not my current path. What had been arising was the deep fear of once and for all releasing my plan B's and fully embracing what was given by the Spirit, which was David. I felt more and more joyous as I continued to follow Bill, and by the time we arrived at his property I was excited to share the good news!

I called David and said, "I'm coming!" He was just as happy as I was. The next day I began a glorious three-day drive back up to Auckland. I sang all the way, and I felt as though I were flying!

A Gift of Rest

Our last tour of gatherings was planned for Australia. As the trip approached I felt too tired to go, and that I wouldn't be able to cope. I prayed, hoping to be told that I wasn't meant to go. Not receiving the guidance I wanted, I obediently packed my bag.

David and I arrived at Raj and Suz's lovely home overlooking the Sunshine Coast, and before long we were sharing miracles stories together. Raj had scheduled several local gatherings and workshops, followed by a weeklong tour down the coast. Leaving the house for the first gathering in Brisbane, Raj was concerned about timing. He needed to fill the car with gas, and according to his calculations, driving the speed limit would only leave us ten minutes in which to prepare the venue. That wasn't enough time to set up the sound equipment, chairs, and a resource table. David assured Raj that we would arrive right on time. As we drove, a beautiful teaching poured through David about how Jesus arranges time and space for his miracle workers. Suz, in the backseat next to me, began to giggle with happiness.

Raj shared that he felt responsible as our host and the event organizer, to get us there on time and have everything ready before people arrived. He believed there was no way we could get there early enough for that, but he was open to a miracle! Suz continued to giggle, and before long she and Raj were recounting miracle stories from their adventures on the road. We stopped for gas and the next thing we knew, we were pulling into the carpark.

To Raj's amazement we had arrived at the venue thirty minutes early! He couldn't believe it! It was scientifically impossible according to the world's laws of time, speed, and distance! In pure joy, we set everything up and still had ten minutes to relax before anyone arrived!

The following day I shared with Raj and Suz how full-on the last year had been for me. The weeklong tour was coming up, and Suz was getting ready to stay with a friend. They immediately invited me to stay at their house while Suz was away and Raj and David toured together. Raj had traveled with other spiritual teachers, and he was thrilled at the thought of spending a week alone with David. I felt some guilt about not going, but they were all so supportive that I simply accepted the gift!

It was two days before I could relax and feel worthy of the opportunity to do nothing. Finally I sank into a deep experience of God. I basked in God. I felt so at peace—one with all and so in love—that I knew without a doubt that *everything* had been perfectly planned to bring me to this experience.

I discovered *The Urantia Book* on the bookshelf and as I read the last section, "The Life and Teachings of Jesus," I felt a deeper and more intimate connection with Jesus than ever before. I was deeply inspired by his humility and patience. He knew he had a mission of such magnitude, and yet year after year he said, "It is not my time yet. My Father will let me know when it is my time." I love him so much.

After their tour, David stayed in Sydney to rest, and Raj returned to the house overflowing with love and gratitude for his time with David. He told me that tears of joy had flowed down his cheeks as he drove home. His eyes shone with wonder as he tried to express what the experience meant to him.

I was grateful that my stepping back from the tour was an essential gift, for myself and for Raj. Shortly afterwards, David and I returned to New Zealand.

I Move My Wedding Ring

David was clear that he was going to be staying at Mia and Kevin's house for the rest of our time in New Zealand. I had some clothes there and at Roger and Jackie's house, and I continued to feel split. I felt a subtle and yet constant threat of loss. Because of the presence of fear in my mind, I was not in touch with the presence of love. I was devastated to find that I was no longer in love with anything, including David.

We had talked through everything many times. There was nothing more to say, and it felt to me that there was nothing more we could do together. I couldn't go any deeper until I had released what I needed to, and there was nothing more David could do to help me. I felt as if I had nothing to give—no inspiration, freshness, or depth to offer within our relationship until I had moved through this phase of letting go. Not knowing what else to do, I shared with David one night that I needed to step back from the marriage. We lay together in prayer, and I slipped my ring from my left hand to my right.

David held me while I cried. He assured me that this love was eternal and that he would be with me no matter what. It felt soft, and I took comfort in knowing that I had done everything I could to keep up with David and stay with the Spirit's plan. After all, I had only been a Course student for two years!

Stepping Back and Letting Go

Seven months of travels and gatherings came to an end. Although I was staying on in New Zealand, and David was returning to the U.S., we remained deeply joined in our shared purpose. I wasn't entirely sure of where I might be living next week, but everything felt right. I saw clearly that the purpose of returning to New Zealand with David had not been about helping me move from one country to another—it was much bigger than that. It was to support me in unwinding from my self-concept and the deep attachments that were holding me back from knowing myself as Spirit and being truly free. I knew I couldn't return to the U.S. unless my heart was fully in it and I could take my next steps with David in joy.

Taking David to the airport felt surreal. On some level I knew this was supposed to happen, but my heart didn't feel full or complete. I was in the depths of a healing process. What did feel clear was that freedom and spaciousness were being given now to allow what was coming next to reveal itself.

Chapter Twenty

Fear of Loss
and the Source of Love

Spring 2006

No words can express God's love for His Son
This Love is what we are,
what we give and receive continually.
Sink into My love for you.

This experience is that which you were seeking,
All problems and plans fade from awareness,
And disappear in the love that we are

Keep coming here, remembering God,
It is here, I am here
for you always,
Awaiting your return.

Love Does Not End

David was back at the Peace House in Cincinnati, and although I felt a reprieve from the intensity of being together, I knew in my heart that I belonged with him. Over the following weeks we spent a lot of time on Skype video calls. Sometimes we had deep talks; at other times we were together in silence as we wrote emails and handled various ministry functions. In some ways it felt as if we were physically together at the Peace House.

My fear that I could actually separate from David was being dissolved. I was seeing that whether our bodies were together or not, our shared purpose continued. This was deeply reassuring.

Fear of Loss

Journaling

Kirsten: Good morning, Holy Spirit. Please help me get clear about my feelings. When David was here I was in fear and resistance; I was not in touch with love at all. Since he left, my fear has been healed at a deeper level, and I am back in the experience of God's Love. But now I am afraid of losing David! David is the presence of God's Love. Everyone is free to love him and be in touch with the same love that is within them. However, when he told me that a friend in Europe had expressed that she is in love with him and wants to marry him, I felt shocked that I could lose him—that our marriage could be over. I feel like I'm still reeling, and I'm tempted to act on it.

Holy Spirit: I've told you many times that you are still married to David and he isn't going anywhere. He isn't leaving. There is a part of your mind that accepts this and a part of your mind that rejects this. The illusory nature of the ego mind insists on imagining the future—painting it either rosy and bright or doubtful and dark. When both are painted onto the same imaginary future, confusion reigns. Every time you have rejected the thought of marriage with David, you have been in fear. The imagined projections have involved loss, lack, and sacrifice. I tell you now there is no loss, lack, or sacrifice in love.

Kirsten: Yes. I was also holding on to alternative plans in case God's plan fails. I know that my family would take care of me if you didn't. Roger would be there in a heartbeat, offering practical and financial support. Jackie would always be there to join me, whatever the adventure—from getting our hair done to exploring the idea of owning a retreat center. New Zealand would always be there, too, a safe spacious country where I would be supported by government loans and medical subsidies if I needed them. Oh my

God, when I write it all out I see how much of a backup plan is still in my mind! No wonder I couldn't genuinely talk about divine providence when traveling with David! I don't really believe that I am supported by you!

I am ready to let all of my backup plans go now. [I sob with relief.] I know I struggled with David because he exposed my plan B's; he was a threat to them. He told me to let them go and I wouldn't. I didn't feel ready.

What else can you tell me about this? I want to be with David, but I don't want to act out of fear now. I know I'm not special, and that he is married to everyone. I don't want to miss the opportunity to join him fully without fear, without the old resistance.

Holy Spirit: Keep exposing the fears and the desires. Remember your one goal: God. Remember your one desire: God. I will guide you. You are exactly where you are meant to be. Yes, you cancelled your return ticket to the U.S. and stepped back from the marriage—and there was fear and confusion involved. However, as I have told you, you are still married; you are still joined with David. You are staying in one place as you wanted. You're letting go of alternative plans and allowing the past to be cleared away. This is making straight your path, leaving no stones to trip on and no obstacles to bar your way. All is well, my child, all is well.

Kirsten: Thank you. [I sigh with relief.]

True Marriage

Journaling

Kirsten: Good morning, Holy Spirit. When I'm in my right mind, all is well. I know that only the ego looks back and judges, hypothesizing about how it could be different. When I'm in my wrong mind, I blame others because their expectations of me were too high. I feel sad because I feel that I failed at being in relationship with David, and then I get angry because it's not my fault! This is followed by feelings of guilt, anger, and disappointment: *I should have done it differently. I'm innocent! Poor me.* I would like to let this go now. What can you tell me? I have the feeling you're going to talk to me about marriage.

Holy Spirit: You are and will always be in union with God. This is true marriage. In the world of form, two people may join together in purpose in a marriage to symbolize the desire to be married with God.

The ego's idea of marriage involves specialness. The Spirit's use of marriage is healing the mind and demonstrating the unconditional Love of God to each other and to everyone. True marriage is beyond form. True marriage is the love, joining, shared purpose, and the feeling of "no separation" that you have, and will always have with David. This was the intention of your relationship and so it is.

Kirsten: I feel and know this. I will trust this. I still seem to feel sad and close to tears. Do I have unconscious thoughts that I need to look at, or is it just that I'm getting caught up in ego wrong-mindedness?

Holy Spirit: Allow the thoughts and emotions to surface. Joining is always the answer to feelings of loss and separation. When you realize that your mind is looping in negative ego thinking, change the subject by deciding for me. Come to me. Sit with me. Express the thoughts with the willingness to let them go with finality.

Kirsten: Thank you. Anything to read?

Holy Spirit: "Do not look back except in honesty. And when an idol tempts you, think of this: There never was a time an idol brought you anything except the 'gift' of guilt. Not one was bought except at cost of pain, nor was it ever paid by you alone. Be merciful unto your brother, then. And do not choose an idol thoughtlessly, remembering that he will pay the cost as well as you. For he will be delayed when you look back, and you will not perceive Whose loving hand you hold. Look forward, then; in confidence walk with a happy heart that beats in hope and does not pound in fear." T-30.V.10

Kirsten: Perfect.

The Son of God Never Slept

Journaling

Kirsten: Good morning, Holy Spirit.

[I feel at peace and am guided to read the last two paragraphs of "Finding the Present" in the Course.]

"The attraction of light must draw you willingly, and willingness is signified by giving. ... The laws of love are not suspended because you sleep. ... Even in sleep has Christ protected you, ensuring the real world for you when you awake. In your name He has given for you, and given you the gifts He gave. God's Son is still as loving as his Father, continuous with his Father, he has no past apart from Him. So he has never ceased to be his Father's witness and his own. ... And so it is that he can call unto himself the witnesses that teach him that he never slept." T-13.VI.12-13

Kirsten: Tell me about this!

Holy Spirit: The Son of God never was separated from his Father. The Son of God seemed to sleep, to forget his Father's Love, to believe he was separate—a body in space and time searching for his purpose, searching for his home. This perception was corrected immediately by me. As you stay devoted to the truth, witnesses will reflect the truth back to you. As you give all to all, loving as your Father loves, witnesses will reflect this Love to you. Gone is the wisp of a dream that anything but love and light are all there is.

In God's Love, everything unlike His Love has vanished without a trace. In the light of His Love, all darkness has disappeared forever. Can the Son of God ever really have been anywhere but here, being that he is unlimited, that he is his Father's Creation, that he was made in the image of His Father?

Kirsten: [I sink into a mystical, expansive awareness of truth and connectedness. There is an unspoken knowing that "Kirsten" and all of her fears of separation and making mistakes were part of a dream.

They are unreal because this moment, this Presence is who I am and who I have always been.]

All sense of separation is gone. It is now unimaginable. It never happened at all.

"God's Son is still as loving as his Father. Continuous with his Father, he has no past apart from Him." T-13.VI

Undoing Associations

The belief that I could lose the one that I love, seems to have been a core issue for me since the beginning of time. Prior to finding the Course, Jackie and I explored all kinds of healing modalities together. One day we visited a psychic who used hypnotherapy as a way to access memories from "past lives" to help bring awareness to patterns that may be playing out in this lifetime. I had a vision where I saw several lifetimes playing out like a romantic tragedy in which I lost the love of my life. Either I was killed or my partner and I were separated through terrible circumstances.

The source of my current fear and sadness is my old belief that I could lose the one that I love, and here I am again—this time starring "David" in the lead role. Once again, I feel the same intense emotions and I see that this belief is still unhealed.

I called David and shared my "past life regression experience" and my present feelings of sadness and loss, and he said, "There really isn't a problem." I tried to explain the reality of my problem to him, and again he repeated that he didn't see a problem. He asked if I wanted to continue playing it out. I laughed! In the midst of my sadness and grief, I laughed! Here was my lead role not buying into my suffering and not trying to understand the incomprehensible at all. Instead, he was reminding me of the truth!

At a Course group days later, one of the members shared a story that she'd told every time I'd been to that group. She recounted her experience as a nurse comforting families as a loved one dies. In her attempt to bring them solace she holds the truth in mind and sees the Christ in everyone. I felt agitated. *Why was she repeating this same story almost word for word?* I thought I understood the point of the story, which is to see the Christ in everyone, and I desperately wanted to take this deeper.

Later, when I turned to the Holy Spirit for help, I saw the connection immediately. She was talking about love and loss, love and death, love and grief. In other words, all of the things that I had been believing and holding onto! Bless you, my beloved sister, for repeating this story for me until I finally got it! I sank into a deep process of forgiveness with the Holy Spirit, releasing all of my false associations between love and loss with every person that I could call to mind. I was told, "You can only believe in and experience loss when you identify yourself as one of the characters in the dream."

The song "There Is Only Love" came floating into my mind: "There is only love, love within and without, up and down, all around us." Beautiful! I felt free! Free to love, free to be, free to watch whatever unfolded with joy and trust.

Joy

Journaling

Kirsten: Good morning, Holy Spirit. I've just read the section about Joy in the Manual for Teachers and it says, "Joy is the inevitable result of gentleness. ... Joy goes with gentleness as surely as grief attends attack." M-4.V Talk to me about this.

Holy Spirit: Grief comes from the belief in attack. To believe in loss, that something dear could be taken away or threatened, gives rise to the belief in attack. Where is trust when attack is in the mind? It has disappeared from awareness; it is blotted out entirely. To realize that loss is impossible is the end of fear. Without fear and without the possibility of loss of any kind, peace, gentleness, and joy are experienced.

Kirsten: Talk to me about how joy is a song of gratitude.

Holy Spirit: Joy is the expression of your natural state, of your inheritance. It is given you of God. Peace and joy go hand in hand with gratitude. The realization that you are safe and loved and whole—that there is nothing wrong, that there is no one to fix, that all things work together for good—gives rise to joy. It is only misperceptions that cover over and obscure the eternal song of gratitude of the Son for his Father. Moments of intense gratitude are glimpses of the truth that is always there.

Kirsten: Talk to me about, "And Christ looks down on them in thanks as well." M-4.V

Holy Spirit: This is a metaphor to describe the idea of Christ. This world seems to be linear and horizontal in its approach to learning and progress. As you release these concepts from your mind, opening to the expansive truth, you begin to realize that true ideas are vertical. This is another metaphor, or "stepping stone" idea, to help you out of illusions. Obviously in Heaven, in the absolute, there are no levels. God Is. Christ is an idea in the mind of God. Christ Is. All is one in perfect equality. In this realm, God is the highest idea. You could consider angels and ascended masters to be very high ideas who have access to wisdom not of this world. They are not bound by the laws of this world.

To use the phrase "Christ looks down on them in thanks as well" is describing the highest part of your mind, or the true nature of your Self, looking down in gratitude as you continue to awaken to the truth about yourself. There is only One Mind; therefore, all aspects, realms, ideas, and symbols are reflections of the One Mind. They can seem to look upon each other, to assist each other, to express gratitude to each other. Again, these are all helpful "stepping stone" ideas.

Kirsten: How does this fit with it all being a dream?

Holy Spirit: You are aware that you are dreaming. You are awakening to the truth of who you are and who your brother is. Calling this experience a dream is simply realizing that it is not reality. It is no more complicated than this. Enjoy your dream, knowing that you are utterly loved and utterly safe.

Chapter Twenty-One

New Beginnings

Summer 2006

"Today we celebrate the happy ending to your long dream of disaster. There are no dark dreams now. The light has come. Today the time of light begins for you and everyone. It is a new era, in which a new world is born. The old one has left no trace upon it in its passing. Today we see a different world, because the light has come." W-75.2

Joyous Reunion

I was still in prayer about whether to stay in New Zealand or rejoin David in the United States. Out of the blue, David's friend Lisa invited David, me, and some other friends to her house in Pennsylvania for a weeklong retreat. She was very excited, feeling that it was a very important reunion, and she offered to buy our flights from wherever we were in the world. This was a clear sign.

It felt right. I felt more certain about my path, and more deeply joined with David than ever before. I had been given all of the spaciousness that I needed to clear through core ego defenses and see for myself what it was that I truly wanted. What I wanted was to go where He would have me go. What I wanted was to go ever deeper into mysticism, into the Heart of God, and there was no doubt that my path was with David.

I felt like I was saying yes to God for the first time. I had said yes before, but now I felt like there was nothing to hold me back. Before I left New Zealand, my heart felt full of love and lightness again, as if I had come out into the sunlight and there was nothing left to do but shine.

After a long journey I arrived in Pennsylvania and David met me at the airport. It was a beautiful, happy reunion. When we arrived at Lisa's house, we discovered that she had prepared a room for us as if we were on our honeymoon. The whole universe seemed to be conspiring to bring us together, and this time I was ready for it to be joyful.

People came from all over the world to attend the gathering. It was a pivotal meeting point that the Spirit had arranged for all of us. The sense of community and the joy of being together was felt by all of us. It was clearly a new beginning in a way we could not define, but we trusted that it would become obvious.

The Past Is Gone

The experience of being with mighty companions, reveling in our union with God, was pure joy. We were all so grateful. The sound of laughter was the last thing I heard before falling asleep every night, and the first thing I woke up to every morning.

One morning during the retreat, I was sitting outside by the fire pit across from my new friend Peter, when I had yet another mystical experience. We had just opened our eyes after meditating when the world disappeared into a misty white light. The form of my friend disappeared as light blazed from him, showing me clearly how the "body mask" was a temporary screen. The experience seemed to go on and on, and I allowed myself to surrender completely to releasing the illusion of the world. Everything around us disappeared and all that was left was pure love and light.

After some time, a soft rain began to fall and the world of form gradually came back into my awareness. Everyone had moved inside and gathered around David in the living room. As I went inside David looked up from his chair and saw my big, wide eyes. "Oh, you're having one of those experiences," he said, beaming in recognition. I felt like a child, completely clueless and a little wobbly on my legs. David gently ushered me to sit on his lap and continued right on with a deep discussion with the group, zooming into the topic of accepting the Atonement.

Lisa's devotion to forgiveness was so clear and certain that it's hardly surprising what happened during the retreat. One of her biological sisters had been murdered twelve years ago. The murderer, who had been convicted, had spent the last ten years in isolation on death-row. Lisa took a telephone call one morning from a newspaper reporter who was phoning to ask for reactions to the news that the convicted murderer might be taken off death row. Lisa's first response was, "Good! I don't believe in death. We believe in forgiveness and our life is all about God. It's about releasing the past. It's over. It's gone." The reporter asked if there was another family member there that he could speak to, and Lisa's sister got on the phone. She said, "Our family has forgiven the past. We don't hold onto grievances and I hope he is released from the prison of his mind. I hope he gets this message because he deserves to be free from guilt."

Not long after, Lisa remembered the convicted man's name. It was Freeman May. The month was May, and as far as we were concerned, he was being made a free man! In our eyes and in God's eyes he had been forgiven and released from guilt. It was powerful.

God My Father, Only You

Following the retreat in Pennsylvania, I basked in the afterglow of an incredible week of miracles and joy. I felt so in Love—with David, with God, with life, with every blessed moment. My relationship with David once again reflected the pure, open honesty of my relationship with God. David had several gatherings planned following the retreat, and Lisa invited me to stay and rest at her house for a few days. I sat in silent reflection and this prayer flowed from my heart.

> Today we bask in silence ...
> A hush has fallen across the world.
>
> *I am among the ministers of God*
> This thought radiates from my mind,
> Enveloping the whole Sonship.
>
> *God, my Father*
> *Only You.*
>
> Waves of gratitude ebb and flow
> Across the ocean of One Mind
>
> *God my Father,*
> *Only You.*

innocent children, waking from a dream,
Realizing none of it was real ...

My hand is in Yours,
My eyes turned to You
My heart is given and will forever be true,
To God my Father,
Only You.

I place my life in your hands,
I place my trust in your Word,
I give my Life to You,
And now I am Home.
With You.

There is no journey,
You are my destination
There is nothing else,
You are All.

I am love, I am whole, with You.

And now is the time to laugh and play,
Now is the time to rejoice,
Now is the time to share the good news:
He is here, I am home, I am free.

Angels Show Up

When David and I returned to the Peace House late Sunday night, we were met by an ecstatically happy Tripod and her new brother Sam, neither of whom could stop purring. Around three a.m., I was woken by Tripod leaping onto my chest, unable to contain her love. She was as happy that I was back as I was.

I had been in prayer about getting some help with the Peace House. David and I were away so much, and it felt like it hadn't had a good, solid cleaning for years. Watching Lisa clean up after the retreat at her place had instantly changed the way I felt about housekeeping. She lit candles, put on music, and poured her heart into it. The place literally sparkled when she was finished. Lisa cleaned for God and did it with great joy.

As David caught up on his backlog of emails, I spent two days cleaning in preparation for our visitors Tamara and Jody, who were coming from Tennessee for the weekend. When they arrived, they took us out for a lovely meal. We talked deep into the night about God and relationships. When they retired for the evening, they told us with absolute sincerity that they were there to be helpful. Their heartfelt desire was to help in every way that they could—cleaning, running errands, doing yard work, anything at all. I could hardly believe it. I had thought I would be taking care of them for the weekend, but they were clearly angels sent straight from Heaven in answer to my prayer for support!

The following morning, Tamara, Jody, and I put on rubber gloves and we cleaned, sorted, rearranged, and cleared all day. It was so much fun. Everything felt fresh and brand new. We took a walk that evening and meditated on benches near St. Bernard Church. A figure of Mary stood nearby, her hands in the prayer position, and flower beds all around her.

I felt completely blessed to have family with me everywhere I went. Later, as I sat at my desk answering emails, I heard contented purring arising from under my chair and thought to myself, *All I see is devotion and all I feel is love. It is here, right now, and I am so grateful.*

Beyond Manifesting

Last night, David and I watched the movie *The Secret* with Tamara and Jody. The movie is a fantastic lead-in to realizing the power of the mind and the law of attraction—what we focus on and want is what we receive. A lot of the movie is about manifesting, on *getting what we want* from the world.

This morning I was guided to read from the section, "The Responsibility for Sight" in the Course: "I am responsible for what I see. I choose the feelings I experience, and I decide upon the goal I would achieve. And everything that seems to happen to me I ask for, and receive as I have asked." T-21.II.2

Journaling

Kirsten: Good morning, Holy Spirit. Can you tell me how does this work with "the script is written" and with surrendering to "what is"?

Holy Spirit: The observer is a state of mind in which you know yourself to be beyond the battleground, at one with God, and therefore not at the mercy of the world. Moving from realizing the potential of the mind to taking total responsibility for sight is to bring awareness back to the Source.

To know thyself is to be beyond this world and its temptations entirely. To ask God in every circumstance, "What is your will for me?" is to align with the Spirit and the result will always be for your highest good.

Kirsten: So it's like ABCD ...
A) I have a powerful mind. I affect my world.
B) I can seem to manifest what I want. I am responsible for what I see, think, and feel.
C) I want nothing of this world, only God.
D) Show me the way to God. I give my life over to the Spirit's guidance in every circumstance.

Now I am free. I am one with God because my desire is not split.

Holy Spirit: Remember always that God is Cause, and you, being His Son, are Effect. Without the purpose of forgiveness, the desire to be the "Ruler of the Universe" is an egoic goal. Being "master of my own destiny" can be a helpful stepping stone along the way to realizing the power of the mind, but ultimately one must come to a point of surrender, humility, and acceptance. God is the Father, and the Christ is His beloved creation through which pours His infinite Love and power.

Chapter Twenty-Two

Teach Only Love

Summer 2006

"The Holy Spirit extends and the ego projects. As their goals are opposed, so is the result. The Holy Spirit begins by perceiving you as perfect. Knowing this perfection is shared He recognizes it in others, thus strengthening it in both. Instead of anger this arouses love for both, because it establishes inclusion." T-6.II.4-5

"The only safety lies in extending the Holy Spirit, because as you see His gentleness in others your own mind perceives itself as totally harmless. Once it can accept this fully, it sees no need to protect itself. The protection of God then dawns upon it, assuring it that it is perfectly safe forever." T-6.III.3

Innocence

David and I left for California to spend ten days with friends and hold gatherings at their local center in the San Bernardino mountains.

Journaling

Kirsten: Good morning, Holy Spirit. What can you tell me about my fear that a sister perceives I have attacked her? She may be right. I reacted because what she posted was not, in my view, in alignment with the Course. I felt that she was meant to be upholding a position of being an ACIM teacher, and she was using language and ideas that weren't from the Course. I felt a sense of judgment and self-righteousness, and I probably shouldn't have written to her in that moment. I don't feel good. Am I just playing out the possibility that I am guilty after all?

Holy Spirit: Beloved child, innocence is what you are. Innocence is who you are. Place your innocence in the hands of God and you will remember peace. Place your innocence at the mercy of the world and you will perceive judgment and condemnation.

Project not onto your sister and brother, for then they are no longer your sister and brother but your enemy. Extend only love and you will be assured of your holiness because of your allegiance with God. To question your sinlessness is to question God's Son, which is to question all that I have taught and all that God Is.

Kirsten: Thank you.

Where Is Consistency?

I felt very reassured after receiving the Spirit's loving response about my innocence, but something was arising within my mind; I could feel the ego being stirred up out of its hiding place.

One day as David was talking at the gathering in California, I began to perceive him as inconsistent. He would begin a conversation and by the second sentence he would seem to be contradicting himself. I wanted to jump in and point this out but something stopped me. I watched and listened as our friends also listened, seemingly enraptured in what he was saying. Either they were not noticing how blatantly contradictory everything he said was or they were pretending not to notice. I started to feel like I was going crazy. What was going on?

I sat on the edge of my seat feeling an internal urgency. "David!" I butted in at one point, but when he looked at me, I couldn't find the words to point out what I was seeing. I shook my head and he continued. I had to get out of there. I quietly left the room, got my shoes, and headed out the door. I began walking up the mountain at high speed, and the feeling of intensity around what I had been perceiving increased. I felt an anger stirring within me. How could David be so inconsistent? How could the inconsistent writing from my friend yesterday have been sent out publicly? We were supposed to be an example of consistency. Was I the only one who cared?

The further I walked, the more intense I felt. When I finally reached the top of the mountain, I felt like I was going to burst. I found myself among trees and large rocks, the perfect place to cry out for help. "Holy Spirit!" I demanded, "Where are you? What is going on? Where is the consistency? I want consistency!"

The anger subsided and a wave of sadness arose. As tears fell, I realized it was God I was longing for. It felt so good to realize this, to feel the depth of longing within my heart. I had been expecting consistent behavior from myself, and from the world. Some kind of a teacher self-concept had crept in, which I had been trying to uphold for myself and was then projecting onto others—it was clearly not of the Spirit.

Finally, as I realized where true consistency was found, the light shone on my struggles of the past, and a deep feeling of peace returned to my soul.

I looked around and found myself in the most beautiful place! As I gazed out from my spot on the top of the mountain, I saw several hang gliders in the sky. They were free, soaring, carried silently and effortlessly on the air currents. Tears of gratitude continued to roll softly down my cheeks. I felt a deep stillness within, and I sat watching the gliders for an hour or so. I then felt the prompt to return and share the good news with David.

Commitments Lead to Consistency

Journaling

Kirsten: Good morning, Holy Spirit. I'm deeply inspired by the subject of consistency. What else can you tell me?

Holy Spirit: God is consistent because He does not change His mind. I am consistent because I am the Voice for God. The guidance that you receive from me is always consistent because it is of God; it is in alignment with God.

The ego is inconsistency. This world is a projection of shifting, changing forms. Consistency cannot be found in this world or in the things of this world. As explained in *A Course in Miracles*, those who seek inconsistency in the book will find it, and those who seek clarity will find it. Turn not to form for your salvation; turn instead to me, your guide, the one who knows your highest good in every circumstance.

To feel let down after finding inconsistency in the words, teachings, or behaviors of others is the result of judgment, and the only correction is forgiveness of one's own misperception. Expectations and comparison always lead to disappointment. Only God can provide what it is that you are seeking.

Your responsibility is to accept the Atonement for yourself. To accept the Atonement is to heal and become happy, to return to a God-like state. God is consistent, and by accepting the Atonement, you are releasing ego beliefs and becoming consistent in your thinking. This means that your thoughts, words, and actions will align and become consistent in every circumstance. Remember that consistency is of God. Your commitment is to God, and to listening and following my guidance.

Because I am the one to whom the plan was given, you cannot possibly know the best interests of another. To judge the actions, words, and teachings of another will result in misperceptions. Again I remind you, this is simply another opportunity for forgiveness.

Consistency in this world is impossible because this world is rooted in time. Time is the illusory attempt to fragment eternity. To compare past teachings with present teachings, or to compare what is said in one part of a book, such as *A Course in Miracles*, with what is said in another part of the book, is the attempt to pull separate pieces of information together, judge them, and draw a conclusion from the results of the judgment. Judging the form is insanity; it proves nothing and cannot lead to peace.

The road to peace is forgiveness; it is the undoing of the "I know mind" that thinks it knows how the world should operate, what should be spoken, and how messages should be delivered. This kind of thinking almost always results in the temptation to withdraw, to judge the messenger, and to turn to *separation* as a solution.

Commitments and assignments involving form are a means of practice for your mind training. I will guide you in these commitments. Remember that although the form will change, the content of my teachings and my guidance is always consistent, being of God.

[I wrote to my ACIM friend and shared all of my learning with her. In my humble state, I told her that I wished I hadn't responded to her writing until after I had moved through my own healing. She told me she had also taken the situation into prayer with the Spirit and was very grateful for my call. It was no surprise that we both came to the same realization of where true consistency is found. It is in our purpose of forgiveness, in our innocence, and in God.]

Chapter Twenty-Three

Intimacy Is with God

Summer/Fall 2006

"Let us be glad that we can walk the world, and find so many chances to perceive another situation where God's gift can once again be recognized as ours!" T-31.VIII.9

Sweet Miracles

David and I returned to the Peace House for a quiet two weeks before I left for a month long tour with my friend Carolina from Venezuela. It was the first time I would be touring with someone other than David, and he was in full support.

One Sunday morning, David and I took a morning walk around the neighborhood. As we passed by the big St. Bernard church, we heard excited whispering, "Look! There are some people!" A woman and a group of young children were sitting down in the shade near the sidewalk. They were shining with happiness and were obviously about their Father's business. We slowed down as we approached them, and one of the young girls walked up to us very slowly, carrying a loaf of bread as if it were a ring on a cushion being presented at a ceremony.

They were giving away loaves of bread with a piece of paper taped on to each loaf. The message said "Awesome God," followed by the story about Jesus multiplying the loaves and fishes to feed everyone who came to be with him.

How beautiful. They were so happy to give us a gift and celebrate our shared love of God. The littlest boy jumped up and down behind a bush, waving and grinning as we joined in a chorus of "Yay God!" with big smiles. Needless to say, breakfast that morning was toast and jam—delicious!

Creator of My World versus Being the Observer

I read a few pages of a spiritual book and found myself confused.

Journaling

Kirsten: Good morning, Holy Spirit. The Course teaches that the ego projected the world. This book says that we are the creator of our own universe and the God of our own experience.

Holy Spirit: You are responsible for your thoughts. Your thoughts become your experience and everything you experience is what you have asked for. Understanding cause and effect is realizing that the thinker and the thoughts are the same. There is no objective world out there.

Kirsten: How does being totally responsible for everything I see fit with the idea of being the dreamer, who is unattached and able to discern truth from illusions? Being creator of my own universe seems proactive, whereas being the observer seems to involve stepping back and watching the screen, remaining unaffected by the ways of the world.

Holy Spirit: The question you are asking is "Who is the I?" The mind training process of *A Course in Miracles* takes you through an unraveling of who you thought you were and what you believed was true. The self-concept, the little I, believes itself to be in the world, one of six billion others, living its own life. It is beginning to realize that it was wrong—it is not at the mercy of the world.

The observer state is one of coming back into the mind, to the experience of oneness and invulnerability. Identification is with God, not with the self-concept and its body. In coming back to the experience of being the observer, you must realize the power of the mind, through the medium of miracles. You must realize the connection between thoughts and experience.

Kirsten: I feel like I'm the observer much of the time, happily flowing along, watching Kirsten go about her Father's business. But occasionally I feel I must be proactive; I think that I could improve the dream for myself—and having a powerful mind, surely I can! [I smile as I realize my thought.]

Holy Spirit: The question to ask is "What do I want?" The moment you consider the dream to be real and try to improve it, you lose awareness of being the observer.

Kirsten: Yes. I am again thinking I know what would be better for myself and my life. I have taken my total trust and faith out of God's hands and put it in my own.

Holy Spirit: As always turn to me for guidance in all matters.

One with God

Today I walked in the Spring Grove Cemetery, and although I go there every few days, today I felt as if I was seeing it for the first time. I was overwhelmed by the beauty. The Love of God was reflected everywhere, and I was moved to tears. Walking around a lake, huge, brightly colored fish came to greet me as I passed. I'd never seen fish like this before—one was the deepest buttercup yellow; another was the brightest orange I had ever seen. A squirrel led the way as I crossed a stone bridge, bounding ahead and pausing to look back at me every few leaps.

Stopping under the shade of a beautiful tree, my eyes fell upon a sign with the name of the tree, "Carolina Allspice." I burst into laughter—it was a fun reminder of my friend, and it made me feel that I couldn't be any more connected than this.

Taking a blanket from the car, I headed for a shady spot near another lake. Shortly after sitting down, a huge fish swam very close by. Three Canada geese descended on the lake, swimming towards me in perfect unison. Their heads were held high, and they moved gracefully. I extended love to them all, knowing that I was extending love to myself. I closed my eyes and basked in the peace. As I reopened them the geese had disappeared and a turtle had arrived. With its head out of the water and mouth wide open, it was looking straight at me.

Returning to the Peace House, I felt so completely connected, knowing that everything was within my mind. My heart was full to overflowing.

I knew that being alone was truly impossible. Being one with God, one with all that is, is the only thing that's real.

Carolina arrived from Venezuela a week later, and we traveled together throughout Florida and California. It was so joyous to be with her, immersing in the music and movement, permeated with the clarity of the teachings of ACIM. During our time together I was experiencing a welcome break from the intensity of the undoing of specialness. The whole trip felt very light, as if I were on a retreat. It was a beautiful gift.

Going beyond Interpersonal Relationship

After my tour with Carolina, David and I were offered a cabin in the woods and I looked forward to spending a quiet week alone together. It was very rare to have unstructured time to ourselves and I imagined it would be deeply restful—little did I know what I was in for. It turned out to be anything but restful for me. However, it was the perfect time to go through a very deep healing.

My relationship with David had become an idol in my mind, and I'd been trying to hide this fact from myself as I feared losing him. Whenever he spoke about visiting and supporting friends, I immediately felt threatened, and wanted to know if he was referring to a man or a woman. If it was a man, I felt relaxed and loving. If it was a single woman, I felt a distinct lack of welcome in my mind. Apart from when we were teaching, I felt the strain of knowing that I was not fully joined with David in the truth. I didn't feel wholly loving towards him, myself, or anyone else while such unloving thoughts were hiding in my mind.

I don't know when it started happening, but I'd begun to think of the Peace House as *my* house, and David as *my* partner, and I felt protective of them both. I felt as if the walls were closing in. The relationship with David had shifted in my mind from one of pure love to one of attachment and specialness. What I considered *my* relationship was no longer holy relationship. David and the Spirit were both guiding me to let go of the idol of David and turn to the Spirit within as my true source of love.

David couldn't join me in the state of mind I was in because there was no true love present within it. I knew David wouldn't say our relationship was over because beyond the specialness that I was stuck in, he knew our relationship was eternal. My deep fear of losing David was preventing me from seeing clearly. I turned to the Holy Spirit in prayer.

Journaling

Kirsten: Good morning, Holy Spirit. Please help me with the concepts of intimacy and partnership.

Holy Spirit: Intimacy is with God.

Kirsten: You know all that is going on in my mind and you know the prayer of my heart. Please help me get clear about this.

Holy Spirit: Partnership is a step. In oneness there is no partnership. Partnership implies two. In this world, it is helpful to use the symbol of partnership until it is no longer useful.

Kirsten: So David is beyond partnership and I'm not. I want to be in partnership, so what's the point? If everything beyond the veil of illusions is God—and I am everything—why do I have to continue in this dream? Once I know the truth, why stay in form? I don't want to be here.

Holy Spirit: [Silence]

Kirsten: I want my relationship with God. I want my relationship with David. I don't want jealousy, defense, attack, or specialness. I am willing to choose the miracle.

[I was guided to turn to Workbook Lesson 264 in the Course, "I am surrounded by the Love of God."]

Kirsten: Holy Spirit, speak to me.

Holy Spirit: My child, what would you have me say?

Kirsten: Speak to me of love, certainty, security, safety, and belonging.

Holy Spirit: You are calling for God.

Kirsten: Can He hear me?

Holy Spirit: I hear you.

Kirsten: If it is God I am calling for, why can't He hear me? Why can't He lift me in His arms right now and hold me forever? You have used the symbol of David to hold me and help me feel safe, but I can't count on the form. Do I have to go beyond it? If so, how?

Holy Spirit: I am the how.

Kirsten: I've tried desperately to hold on to David and it's hell. I don't want this. It's not love; it's fear. How do I become God-dependent when David is with me? How do I deal with this and not try to keep it to myself? What if I'm left with nowhere to turn?

Holy Spirit: Do you trust me?

Kirsten: Yes.

Holy Spirit: Trust in me through David.

Kirsten: But he's not God.

Holy Spirit: Again I ask—do you trust me?

Kirsten: Yes.

Holy Spirit: Then trust in me through David. Don't judge his motives or thinking. He is your brother and mighty companion, a symbol in your mind. He is taking steps with you, guiding you home with total devotion to God. Raise the bar. This is what you have spoken of to others; now it is time that you do the same. Lift your mind; raise it higher above this earthly realm of interpersonal relationship and behavior-based thinking. You are so far beyond this. You are so much more than this. Do not allow your holy mind to sink into illusions. This is your choice, given you of God.

Kirsten: What will become of the life of Kirsten? Where is this headed in form? Am I to be a traveling mystic or to be settled in one base? Will I stay with David? I'm afraid.

Holy Spirit: God is Life. There is no life in form. To ask questions such as these is to attempt to kill the Christ. You are the way, the truth, and the life. You cannot measure life in terms of symbols; they are meaningless in and of themselves. Give your fears and doubts to me, and be completely and totally intolerant of mind-wandering, this is unworthy of you. You are the holy, eternal, child of God. Accept your inheritance now. Raise up *now*. Enough of playing small and vulnerable—release the witnesses of doubt. Release the symbols of fear and form. Release all future concepts and past concepts. They are not who you are.

Clinging to Relationship

I am guided to read the "Beyond All Idols" section in the text. T-30.III The notes I jot down feel like poetry:

> Thoughts seem to come and go, but
> Thoughts of God are beyond change.
> The Thought God holds of me is like a star,
> He is the sky embracing and holding me.
> Beyond all idols is the Thought God holds of me,
> Surrounded by stillness,
> Resting in certainty and peace.

Journaling

Kirsten: Good morning, Holy Spirit. Finally I am resting in peace. Please talk to me about giving all in total trust versus withholding.

Holy Spirit: Your choice is always between love and fear. Your reasoning is either fear-based or given. Sacrifice is always of the ego. Give freely and you can only receive more. Withhold and you will experience and witness withholding. You have always been provided for. You always have enough—more than enough. I am always with you.

Embrace your life fully. Plans have been given you. Embrace them, move forward with them, enjoy them. Use what resources are given you; that is what they are for. Only belief in the ego and listening to doubt thoughts can hold you back from total happiness now. Kirsten does not have all of the answers; she is given what she needs to know moment by moment.

Kirsten: Last night when David talked about the nothingness of relationship based on the ego, I took it personally. I feel like everything is temporary now and I don't really know what to commit to.

Holy Spirit: David is one who is devoted to awakening and will not be delayed. He expects nothing less of you. His devotion is to God. His love is of God and for God. Kirsten cannot possibly fulfill his desire. At any moment that your desire is for any love other than God's, a false idol has been mistakenly chosen and must be released.

To be with David is to be totally devoted to God, to awakening. This means total devotion to giving all in mind; there is no room for withholding, and the withholder is not part of God's plan. When you identify with the withholder, you feel the temporary nature of the ego, the lack of integrity and commitment. Of course you feel as though you are on shaky ground—you have chosen to separate yourself from God, as if doing so could provide safety and security when all you want is to be One with God.

Protectionism is simply another mask. You can let it go now. It was a misperception to believe that it could bring you closer to God. In worldly terms, *saving for a rainy day* is sensible. In God's terms, in terms of awakening, you must place all of your faith, trust, and devotion in my hands. In terms of form, this means giving freely as guided and using what I have given you to serve my plan.

This Is about You and Me

Journaling

Kirsten: Good morning, Holy Spirit, out of the blue, the attachment to New Zealand is up again this morning. What is going on?

Holy Spirit: Trust. The plan will be given you moment by moment. Just as with releasing specialness with persons, you must first let go. How can I give you the real world when you are holding onto the old one? Trust. You must be in integrity. You must demonstrate honesty and trust. You must demonstrate giving all; in doing so, you will learn of God. Holding on to anything of this world is the belief in death. Your motivation must be of God, not of fear and protectionism. How can I give you what you want when you are holding on to what you don't want with both hands? You must untie yourself. Free your mind.

This is not about David or location. This is about you and me. This is about God. This is about ending the cycle of fear and death. The only thing in need of protection is the mind. To attempt to protect yourself as a body is choosing to remain in the cycle of death. The script of the world is death. The release from the ego's script is life, God, awakening. The way is to trust in me. Awakening is total, not partial. You have come a long way and there is no turning back. You cannot turn back to death. That is simply not an option.

[My mind was swirling with thoughts of desperately wanting to have a normal life in the world. The ego was raging, and then—like a bubble—it popped. Sadness arose as I said farewell to any remaining hope of an interpersonal relationship. I had finally made the decision to release the desire for relationship as I knew it, and to trust. Light returned to my mind.]

I felt so silent. No words, no stories to tell, no associations with the past or anything of this world. Detached, in the void.

Detached in a Good Way

It had become clear that David and I were no longer to be marriage partners, although we were still to travel and teach together. Flying to Philadelphia with David for a gathering, I had no idea how it would go as I felt so utterly detached from everything. I had nothing to say. When our hosts collected us at the airport, a gentle love and peace began flowing through my mind. Although I felt deeply quiet, the Spirit poured through me that evening, using many parables and teachings from my recent experiences. I felt connected to the deep, vast, experience of God, and completely unattached to the world. It was as if Kirsten had left the building.

Beyond specialness and interpersonal relationships,
Above the fear of death and loss,
Beyond the desire to withhold and protect,
Is God.
Only in God can certainty, security,
Safety, love, and peace, be known.

Deep in the quiet stillness of mind
Is the Father's Love for His Son.
Extending forever,
I am my Father's beloved child.
I am my Father's Love.

On the Other Side

Love, peace, and gratitude radiate throughout my whole being. The idea that any mistakes have been made in the past is incomprehensible. I know that everything was planned by One who loves me, to bring me to this awareness. The opening to love, including the attachment to symbols, has played out perfectly. The Spirit used the symbols to take me beyond them.

So am I in love now? Oh, yes. The love that I am is so vast and all-encompassing. There is nowhere that love is not. My love is not attached to form and so it cannot be lost. All wisps of anxiety and pain have gone, dissolved away in the light of truth. The idea of loss is now impossible, laughable.

I am so deeply grateful to God, to the Spirit, and to every blessed reflection of the Love of God that has helped bring me here to abstraction. I am free.

Dancing in light, singing His praises, basking in God ... Amen.

Chapter Twenty-Four

I Am Calling You out of the World

Fall/Winter 2006

Listen carefully throughout the day.
Praise God by loving His Son.
Praise God by raising your mind
to the heights of Heaven
and addressing each brother with love.
Praise God by offering each brother
the opportunity to join.
There is no greater service
that you can offer the Lord.

Angels, Trucks, and Mystics with Shovels

David and I have been feeling how helpful it would be to have some administrative and domestic support. Our prayer was answered in the form of Charles, a Course student we'd met at a gathering. He wrote saying that he'd like to live at the Peace House and help with cooking, cleaning, and administration. It was everything we needed help with. Charles also offered the full amount of his monthly pension, which covered the Peace House expenses exactly!

After a couple of months with us, he made a donation that was the amount needed to purchase a car and a hot tub. David often talked about the Greeks having deep discussions in their warm pools. I loved the idea of soaking outside under the trees, watching the birds and squirrels.

After some investigation we discovered that the cost of building a base for the tub was very expensive. Willing to be shown, we gave the project over to the Spirit for direction. The following weekend, we saw a moving sale that listed everything from vehicles to building materials. We arrived in time for the car auctions and, after several bids, my arm shot up in the air. Looking at David, I said, "What is happening?" Just go with it," David replied. "Nine-hundred dollars from the lady," the auctioneer said, looking at me. Another bidder offered nine-hundred-and-fifty dollars, and the auctioneer looked at me again. I motioned "no," but he took it to mean yes. I was clearly not in control of what was happening! Attempting to tell the auctioneer that I had said no, my words were spoken so softly that no one but David heard me. The auctioneer continued to include me in the bidding, "Twelve-hundred dollars! Sold to the lady in the blue fleece!" Apparently, I had bought a white pickup truck!

The owner of the vehicle, Mike, came over and congratulated us on buying such a great truck. We told him that we were actually there for some bricks since we were going to try and build a hot-tub base. We got to talking with Mike about our ministry and living a life of trust. We shared that we were letting the Spirit guide us where to go and what to do, because we had no idea how to build the base. Mike's eyes began to sparkle. Over the next few hours, between cups of tea and talks about his desire for faith and forgiveness, he filled the back of our new truck with everything we needed to build a solid base. He told us in detail how to build the base and loaned us the equipment and tools we would need. He joyfully donated bricks, cement, pavers, and sand. Mike's faith in God was restored and we were all in such joy!

We drove home in our new truck, loaded with love, gratitude, bricks, and mortar. Oh, what a glorious plan of the Spirit! In the following weeks we worked outdoors, making the base and a patio area. Charles often watched from the kitchen window as David and I were happily building. He was surprised to see mystics shoveling sand and laying pavers. He thought that his arrival would free us up from practical tasks so that we could focus on our communication functions! It certainly was an unexpected project, and we thoroughly enjoyed the change of pace. We found ourselves laughing about how backdrops were all the same when in the joy of the Spirit—from traveling to counseling to lifting bricks.

In Competition with God

We took another road trip to Florida where David had a series of gatherings planned. In the midst of them, the thought *I want to speak* began arising within me again—this time with a vengeance. It was the same as the *I'm nothing more than an accessory to the mystic* experience in Argentina, but more intense.

Shortly into each gathering I felt impatient and underused. Left unchecked, the ego began judging David for not letting me speak. In my perception, the Spirit poured through David, hardly pausing at all, and I would speak perhaps once or twice, very briefly. Immediately after every gathering, David would turn to me with a big smile and say, "That was wonderful!" *Agh!* I didn't want to burst his bubble and tell him what was going on in my mind.

Many people came to me after the gatherings and told me that what I'd said was essential for them to hear. I would be bathed in gratitude, remembering that I'd been of service to the Spirit. But during the actual gatherings, what was arising within me was anything but gratitude and joy.

Keeping secrets was not an option, and so I shared my thoughts with David. He listened and shared a beautiful teaching with me about how none of it was personal. I was so grateful to receive his loving response. He told me the Spirit was in charge of everything, including the speaking. I sensed that he was speaking to something beyond my current level of understanding, and I was very receptive to what he was saying.

I prayed late into the night. I looked at all my familiar attack thoughts about David talking too much, me not having a chance to speak, the prideful thoughts that I could have said it better, and the unworthiness thoughts that I didn't know what to say. It still felt very personal. Finally, I dropped beneath the surface thoughts. I could immediately feel what the core belief was: competition. I was in competition with David. The ego was in competition with God! No wonder David didn't give me too much airtime at the gatherings. With all of this going on, I was not a clear channel for the Spirit to pour through.

My prayer turned to, "Spirit, show me how this isn't personal. Show me that the same Spirit that is in David is in me." I felt so happy to know that I was experiencing competition. Now I had something to work with as soon as the feelings and thoughts arose. Thank God! No more sitting in front of an audience wishing to have a different experience. I could now stay focused on the purpose of forgiveness, without judging my experience. This was truly all I wanted. More than being *the speaker*, I wanted the strength and certainty of knowing that I was where I was meant to be. I wanted to be in my holy purpose, connected with the Spirit.

In prayer in the early hours of the morning, I received a beautiful teaching from the Spirit flooding through my mind. The following night at the gathering, after David introduced us, the entire teaching I had received from the Spirit the night before poured from his lips. I sat there in absolute joy! Oh, to be shown that there is only one mind! One Spirit!

David was a clear channel for the Spirit to pour through, so of course he was the one who served as the conduit. I was back in the love and in total gratitude.

Entitlement and Fear of Loss

Ever since my recent week of letting go of interpersonal relationship, I noticed that my mind went back and forth about my relationship status with David.

When intensity or pride came up and I felt resentful towards David or the ministry, I watched my thoughts of wanting to push him away, glad that I wasn't "in a relationship" with him anymore. On the flip side was the sneaky feeling of wanting to present us as still being together to the world. Sharing postings on the mailing list about coming events, I felt a subtle feeling of egoic satisfaction every time I wrote our names together. I had to admit to myself that this was the image I wanted to present to the world. I didn't want anyone else to know that we weren't "together."

A visitor came to stay at the Peace House for a couple of weeks. The only thing she was drawn to was meditation, and at first I welcomed her and her desire for stillness. However, after a while I started to resent her for not helping around the house. I also felt a sense of personal entitlement growing. I was invested in maintaining the image of a self who was important. I could justify my "important" position at the Peace House, whereas our new visitor was receiving our support to simply sit in meditation.

One afternoon David began talking about divine providence and how everything was provided beautifully by the Spirit. He happily told her that we didn't own anything, and that everything—the Peace House, the hot tub, and all of our resources—were to serve all of us equally. These remarks reminded me of our experience in Colombia, when he had said he was married to everyone, including Lili and her mother!

My mind became crowded with troubling thoughts: *I have worked hard for all of this. I have carefully stewarded money. I have traveled all around the world and been through so much. I have even laid down the pavers for the patio! I have devoted my whole life to this, and now I see that all of my work has just been given away.*

I returned to the sanctuary of my room and went into prayer. I remembered the Course's teaching: "Ownership is a dangerous concept if it is left to you." T-13.VII.10 My God, isn't that the truth? My sense of entitlement and self-importance had led me to believe that the Peace House belonged more to me than to those who, in my judgment, had not contributed as much as I had. I truly believed that others could threaten my relationship with God, that I could lose by sharing everything with my sisters and brothers. A deep sadness arose at the thought that I'd failed, that I wasn't loving or healed enough. I felt so little in this identity. I quietly wept and fell into a soft surrender, fully accepting that I had no control over what was happening. All I wanted was to let go of the pain.

Tripod Answers the Call

Late one night I was feeling a deep sadness at the thought of losing David. Alone in my bed, I was silently calling out for love in my mind. Tripod telepathically hearing my call, came bounding up the stairs, only to find my bedroom door was shut. Not to be stopped, the door flew wide open, and she somersaulted into my room, her legs fully outstretched! As she stood up I heard her "Meow!" as if to announce that everything was fine now that she was there. She hippety-hopped across the floor and leapt onto my bed, purring like a tractor, and rubbing all over my hand with such intense love, that I couldn't help but giggle. She stayed with me all night, purring every time I moved. I felt the Love of God returning to my mind, and I resolved to keep my heart open, no matter what.

Let Go and Stay with the Love

The following morning, I shared with David how much sadness I felt about us no longer being a couple. David reminded me of the prayer that I'd begun my journey with. I had wanted to experience a love that couldn't come to an end. And this was it. This was the answer to my prayer. This was the answer to no longer playing out losing the love of my life lifetime after lifetime. It was time to end the romantic drama of human existence and instead accept the truth—that true love cannot come to an end, that true love is found in the purpose of awakening.

I felt that what David was saying was true, but I could barely grasp the depth of what it meant because I was afraid. David had been with me every moment for two years, supporting me, holding me, catching me, leading me. He was so closely associated with my relationship with God that I simply didn't know if I could sustain it without him. I wondered how I was supposed to let him go and stay in the same house with him.

Clearly, specialness was once again rising up in my mind to be healed. I was afraid of being replaced, and so I prayed for guidance. I asked Jesus where he would have me go, and waited for his reply. But he didn't say a thing. I asked if I was supposed to go to New Zealand or out to Kansas to visit with our friends, but again his response was silence. I was not to leave.

I watched my mind wanting to justify the desire to protect myself from pain by pulling away from David. Each time this started to happen, I would catch it and go straight in his direction instead. He welcomed me with open arms, and I would curl up and cry. It always felt so good to be held in the arms of love rather than pulling away into the darkness in a crazy attempt to use separation as a solution.

Without the symbol of our marriage in place, I could see what was underneath it and how invested in it I had become. The symbol had become my identity, and I believed I would be lost without it.

I Am Calling You out of the World

When I first started studying the Course I had a close relationship with Jesus. It was as if Jesus had written each Workbook Lesson specifically for me, as if the ink was still wet on the page. But now I was so preoccupied with the fear of losing David that my relationship with Jesus was sometimes almost forgotten. I longed for the deep connection to return. I went deeply into prayer over the following weeks, and it was during this time that my relationship with Jesus deepened more than ever. I was up at all hours of the night, praying in the candlelit sanctuary. I had long dialogues with Jesus, pouring out my thoughts and fears, while looking into the eyes of a picture of him. One night he told me something that had me sobbing in gratitude and recognition, "I am calling you out of the world—you just didn't know what this meant before."

The Miracle Surrounds You in Every Heartbeat

Journaling

Kirsten: Good morning, Holy Spirit. Speak to me of love.

Holy Spirit: My beloved child, I am always with you. I can never leave you. Only your doubtful thoughts can seem to block my voice from your awareness, but you always come back to me. It is your will, and your will is strong. You are never alone. I am always with you, guiding you step by step.

Pay close attention to each moment and you will notice the love and the miracles that surround you in every heartbeat.

Don't take life for granted. Embrace it. Value it. Give thanks for it. It is the answer to your prayers. You are being guided home, and it is up to you how you feel about it in each moment. You give your blessing to it and it is blessed; you resist it and it seems difficult and fearful. Do not cling to form, to the past, to a belief in lack because something seems to have changed.

Release the repetitive doubt thoughts as soon as they arise. Including the ones about doing—doing next, doing today, doing in four month's time—otherwise your awareness of love and purpose will be blocked.

Come with me, be with me. Love and shine with me. Trust and have faith in me. Allow the past to be washed away in light, love, and gratitude. Now is your moment of release. Now is the holy instant in which you are the holy child of God, joined in an eternal love, never again to believe in separation. That was a mistake. That is not what your holy brother is for. He is with you to witness to love, truth, and eternity. He will not leave you. It is not his will.

Allow regret to be washed away. It couldn't be any other way. You didn't do anything wrong. The mind is healing. All that matters now is love. Put all of your faith in God, in the Love of God through your brother. No matter where you are or where you go, I am always with you. You are never alone. All things work together for good, without exception. Do not try to figure anything out. Let it be revealed to you.

Return to Love

After so much healing around specialness, I wrote this Christmas message from my heart:

We are the love that we feel, witness, and reflect. To see with the eyes of Christ is to know yourself truly, as love. The idea of a *special someone* is an ego concept; it is the attempt to project specialness and love onto form. To mourn the loss of form in one's life is to mourn an illusion. Love has no object. Love cannot be contained within a body. Be glad that this is so.

Love is. Love abounds and is content. Love is who we are. A common ego belief is that people can love each other. If this were true, then separation would be real. The return to God's Love is the forgiveness of illusions, the forgiveness of the ego's illusory version of love, and of the belief in separate people.

Love is simple, love is kind. Love is natural, love is present. Love is an experience of joy. Love is the absence of fear, and the result of releasing illusions. To cling to an image, a relationship, a memory of the past, no matter what name it is given, has nothing to do with real love.

Joyful, loving memories are reflections of a love that is always present. Only devotion to God in the present moment opens the mind to the experience of love now. I thank God from the depths of my heart that nothing needs to change for love to be known. I thank Jesus with all of my being for showing me the way to an experience of real love that can never end.

Blessings of love, peace, and joy to you throughout the Christmas Season. May the pure and shining, innocent awareness of Christ—your holy Self—be in your awareness in every blessed moment.

Chapter Twenty-Five
The Script Is Written
Winter/Spring 2007

"... there is no step along the road that anyone takes but by chance. It has already been taken by him, although he has not yet embarked on it. For time but seems to go in one direction. We but undertake a journey that is over. Yet it seems to have a future still unknown to us." W-158.3

Changeless Love

Jackie invited David and I to hold a retreat in New Zealand. I felt to go a few weeks early to see my family and spend some time on the quiet beaches. Meditating one night with Jesus strongly in my mind, I felt a subtle fear arise. I asked Him for help, and I found myself in the midst of a vision. The vastness of the galaxy surrounded me, and I was suspended in space, holding onto the world; my arms were wrapped around the planet. Jesus appeared in front of me, holding out his arms and saying gently, "Give it to me." I could feel the fear of letting go, "But I will fall," I said, "What will happen to me?"

I realized that I was holding onto the world because I believed it needed me and I needed it. Again Jesus said, "Give it to me now, Kirsten. Let me take care of it." I was still afraid of what would happen to me, but my grip was loosening, and it felt good to finally be letting go. As the world slipped from my arms, I fell slowly backwards. Not into oblivion as the ego would have had me believe, but into the deep, silent ocean of peace within my mind, into the arms of God.

Love and Peace Are the Result of Decision

Journaling

Kirsten: Good morning, Holy Spirit. I will be leaving for New Zealand soon, and I have some pending separation anxiety and sadness. I feel like I've done something wrong, that I don't belong somehow. I feel sad that I will be away from David for six weeks.

Holy Spirit: Do you really?

Kirsten: [The feelings had faded away completely within moments.] Right now? ... No ... it's gone.

Holy Spirit: You released your wrong-minded thinking, which you were experiencing as sadness, with your willingness to turn to me, and now it's gone. David is not your source. I am your source. Turn to me. I will guide you. I have guided you to turn to David many times because the healing that was required was joining with him.

The peace, love, and healing you've experienced have all been the result of following my guidance. Never forget this. David is not the cause of your healing; your decision is. Now is the time to be strong in the Spirit. Now is the time to raise your heart, your love, and your thoughts to always being a teacher of God. You are demonstrating that there is no separation. Your brothers are looking to you for comfort. Be the way-shower that you are. Love attracts love. There is nothing more attractive than perfect love. There is nothing more certain, peaceful, happy, and clear as knowing yourself as love.

Turn to me immediately. You have a wealth of mind training and a multitude of miracles that have paved your way. You cannot fail but for an instant; failure is but a momentary forgetting. I am the thought adjuster and when you turn to me, I will make the adjustment immediately. Walk through this with your heart shining. This is your moment of release. "All power is of God. What is not of Him has no power to do anything." T-11.V.3

A Little More on Love

Over the past weeks, I had been exploring deeper realms of my mind, and allowing feelings of anger to arise. I found twelve pages on the topic of anger in the Course. Twelve! Jesus declares that anger is never justified, and he goes into the subject in great detail. He gives a clear metaphysical context for it, while at the same time making it very clear that there is a misperception and a choice involved. I was aware that I was dealing with a grievance. Although I couldn't have articulated what the grievance was actually about, I could feel resentment that was being projected in David's direction. I thought it had to do with specialness but I couldn't be sure. I couldn't see clearly—all I could do was observe my desire to be right, and turn to prayer for help. I had been through enough dark times to recognize this was a time for faith, and to trust that some deeper healing was taking place.

Finally, my prayers have been answered. This week I felt a distinctive inner shift that is not really describable in words, other than to say it was a surrender into willingness. This morning, I read a beautiful article by David called "Love." The following writing flowed from within me:

Love is all-encompassing innocence,
it comes into awareness upon invitation.
To give as God gives is to know thyself and God.
When something else is desired, love cannot be what it is,
because love cannot be objectified.
To desire "love from another" is to deny love Itself,
and not know one's Self and God.
To return to love is simply to remove
the blocks to love's presence.
To include all in the Love of Christ is absolution.

To see with the eyes of Christ is to bless the world,
to love as God loves, to be One with Him.
Peace, love, joy, and true compassion are Gifts of the
Kingdom, ever present, always available.
Love makes a home, abiding in and including all.
Love makes the whole world sparkle
with joy and happiness.

Cares and concern have gone, trust reigns,
and joy extends with delight, everywhere,
in blessed relationship.

Love is here and love is now.
Love cannot be held onto or anticipated.
Love is ever present, only present,
and radiant presence.

An Image of "The Script Is Written"

"Time is a trick, a sleight of hand, a vast illusion in which figures
come and go as if by magic. Yet there is a plan behind appearances
that does not change. The script is written. When experience will
come to end your doubting has been set." W-158.4

I was in prayer around the teaching from the Course on "the script is
written," when I received a vision and a message from the Spirit. This was
the message:

Imagine that *the script* is a book containing the history of the entire
cosmos and the world, of every lifetime, and that it was written by the ego.
In looking at the pages, you could find your name. The pages of the script
reveal the story of your childhood, the people in your life, as well as your
jobs, situations, spiritual journey, etc.

Clairvoyants seem able to look into the future and accurately describe
what happens because they can read a few pages or chapters ahead. In realizing
that the script is written, does the character Kirsten have control over her
destiny? Does she get to choose what happens in her life? No, of course not.
The ink of the script is dry. The spiritual journey, or the awakening, is the
realization that I am not a character in the book. Forgiveness is the process
of seeing that the ego wrote the script and made up the characters. Each of
the characters in my life is simply playing their role, their assigned part in
the script. When the script seems to play out in a way that is unexpected,
doesn't seem to make sense, or is outright distressing, I must remember that
I am perceiving with the ego. I am trying to make sense of the script from
within the pages. The only way out is to turn to the Spirit and ask to see it
differently, to remember that I don't know what anything is for.

My brothers are innocent, as am I. Through forgiveness, I release them from the belief that they are responsible for what they did. I take total responsibility for my state of mind—for how I perceive and for how I feel about what is playing out. It is in bringing myself back to being the observer that I can choose to watch, as if reading the book, rather than being enmeshed in the story.

Spirit, Divine Mind, is what I am. As I look with the Love of God in my heart, I see a forgiven world. I see the Love of God reflected in the words and the characters. Each blessed page is an opportunity to extend the love that I am.

Think of the Spirit as being an eraser, or white-out fluid. When I look with Him, with His vision, it is as if He has erased the interpretation of what I had written, and the script has been re-written from a place of love.

Since the Script Is Written, Can I Still Have Control?

Journaling

Kirsten: Good morning, Holy Spirit. I don't completely understand what "the script is written" means. If I free my mind of the script, does that mean that I will not be bound by it? I don't like the idea that I don't have control—perhaps I still want to create at least some of my dream the way I want it to be.

Holy Spirit: Who is the "I" that believes itself to be bound in time and space? The "I Am" presence, the Christ, who you truly are, never entered into time and space. Mind does not enter matter.

The script is past; it was over long ago. My voice is the answer to any question that may arise about it. Attempting to escape from the script is another attempt to make the unreal real. Identification as Christ is the answer. The idea of a script falls away in this; it is dissolved in truth.

Kirsten: In the movie, *Mr. Destiny,* the character makes a decision that leads to the circumstances of his life changing. How does the script apply to this? If it is already written, how can he seem to make a decision that affects his life in a different way?

Holy Spirit: It seems there are choices to be made, that you can make a right or a wrong decision. There is always fear around making a wrong decision and that fear is of separation. When a decision is made *alone* by the deceived mind—from a state of unhappiness—the result is a reflection of this decision. There may seem to be temporary relief from making a change in form but mind is still asleep and dreaming of change through improving the circumstances. The only way out is purpose. Turn to me and say, "Decide for God for me," and I will lift your mind above the battleground, out of the script. I will remind you of who you are.

Kirsten: So when I am not identified as a character, and I allow you to guide my thoughts and actions, does life seem to play out differently than how the ego would have directed it?

Holy Spirit: In every moment, you are listening to either my voice or that of the ego. You are perceiving with me or the ego. This is the focus of all mind training and mind-watching. The forgiven world perspective comes from watching with me.

Kirsten: What about form? I don't feel that you've answered my question.

Holy Spirit: You are concerned with the Kirsten character. You are making the body an idol, the central figure of the dream. When you listen to my guidance and you identify as Christ, there is no script.

Kirsten: Ah ... I feel it all releasing ... thank you.

Chapter Twenty-Six

Steadfast Devotion

Winter/Spring 2007

"Vision will come to you at first in glimpses, but they will be enough to show you what is given you who see your brother sinless. Truth is restored to you through your desire, as it was lost to you through your desire for something else." T-20.VIII.1

A Period of Settling Down

"This is a quiet time, in which the teacher of God rests a while in reasonable peace. Now he consolidates his learning. ... The teacher of God needs this period of respite. He has not yet come as far as he thinks. Yet when he is ready to go on, he goes with mighty companions beside him." M-4.I.A.6

My time in New Zealand before David arrived felt very much like the quiet time described in the Manual for Teachers. It was a time of rest. My days were spacious, beginning with journaling, reading, and yoga; flowing into meditations, beach walks, impromptu gatherings, experiential sessions, and deep talks over cups of tea.

It was the *happy learner* phase, where I no longer felt guilty or wanted to hide my private thoughts. Rather, I was a happy detective who knew there was a clue to freedom underneath each upset. I felt certain of my life's purpose, knowing that my path was with David. It was beyond what we were doing or where we were located; it was a feeling of being completely present—no longer aching over loss or the fear of loss, or wishing that I was elsewhere.

When David arrived we held many wonderful gatherings and retreats in New Zealand and Australia. The retreats were held at incredible venues in native forests, with natural swimming holes and forest walks. The meditation rooms were sanctuaries for the heart, perfect for falling into deep stillness, surrounded by a gentle chorus of birdsong and chirping cicadas. The retreats had an intuitive flow. The talks with David were deep, and I felt fully used by the Spirit as a miracle worker during one-on-one talks. I occasionally spoke during the gatherings with David. I also held yoga and experiential sessions with music, dance, and massage.

Much of the competitiveness and self-doubt had been washed away, and I felt content to sit beside David, fully embracing every opportunity to extend. I felt connected with him and with everyone else, feeling the grace of the Spirit flowing continuously. When David turned to me at the end of a talk with a big smile of gratitude, I shone just as brightly.

After each gathering, people came immediately to eye-gaze with me in presence. While the rest of the room was filled with excited discussions and the busyness of packing up, I found myself engaged in deep, silent communion time and time again. It was the most natural thing in the world, ending with twinkling eyes, smiles, and either tears of gratitude or bubbling laughter.

I remember my prayer to the Spirit two years ago, asking what my function was. His reply had been, "You are simply to be the presence of love." How simple, how humble, and yet how glorious it is to know this is my function!

Inspired by Steadfast Devotion

David and I were back in the U.S. and we were invited to Boston to hold some weekend gatherings. While we were there, we went to Cambridge and visited the memorial for Mary Baker Eddy, the founder of Christian Science. Her memorial had a large carved stone with a quote about science being of mind, and God and Spirit being eternal. David occasionally spoke to me of Mary Baker Eddy and her uncompromising nature. I was grateful to be reminded of way-showers who were as unswerving in their devotion as David was. He happily told the parable of how some of her students left after the Spirit boomed through her one day, saying, "I am infallible!"

Mary Baker Eddy was radical; she did not hold back in her message or her willingness to be used fully by the Spirit. Through single-minded devotion, she supported thousands of students in becoming miracle-working practitioners. Despite the lifesaving miracles they experienced, most of her students reached a point where they found her too radical, and they turned against her. David was greatly inspired that in spite of all that seemed to happen, she remained steadfastly devoted to truth. I too was deeply inspired by her example. It was a reminder that our goal of mysticism is not of this world, and is therefore not dependent on approval.

We had wonderful gatherings that weekend where the talks were mostly about holy relationship. After so much letting go of specialness, I was able to share from the perspective that there truly is no sacrifice or loss in saying "yes" to relationship with God. I facilitated an outdoor experiential session based on "The Happy Learner" section of the Course. During part of the session, the group formed a small circle, and we took turns to *be unravelled*, to unlearn everything we had learned, and be returned to truth. Standing in a close circle, we leaned on one another, resting in God. We then merged back into a large circle where we were moved around by the music, looking deeply into each other's eyes. As the final song played, several of us found ourselves in a mystical experience—everything dissolved into white light. I lost track of all sense of being a facilitator, and the session naturally came to an end; some people lay on the grass and others continuing to stand, in long, silent embraces.

Holiness: The Gift of Freedom

Deep within the quiet mind,
I know my Self as holiness.
My holiness is the peace of God.
My holiness blesses the world.
My holiness is the gift of freedom
offered my brother.
In my holiness is his release.
Holiness is the end of guilt and fear;
The past is dissolved in its presence
Even forgiveness has dissolved.
What could there be left to forgive?
This gift of God is salvation accomplished ...
Acceptance was the key.

Final Relinquishment of Plan B

David and I were back at the Peace House, and in prayer with Jesus I asked to be free of anything that was holding me back. I heard the guidance to sell the rental house I owned in New Zealand and immediately donate the funds to the ministry. A year and a half earlier, I had looked at the purpose of continuing to own the property, however I had not taken any steps to actually sell it. At the time I saw that the house was giving me a false sense of security, but I was frightened to tell my family about the decision to sell, as it meant leaving them, and New Zealand, behind for good.

Occasionally over the past year I had seen that when resistance was high in my mind, the house became an alternative to the Spirit's plan. It was something I could *go back to.* Sitting in the presence of the Spirit, I could feel the lightness of the direction to let go of something that was *elsewhere,* and to have every part of my mind where I was. I shared the guidance I'd received with David, and continued on with life at the Peace House.

Weeks later I was feeling separate from David, and I didn't know why. Out of the blue he asked me if the house was for sale yet because the funds from the sale were to be transferred to the ministry. I was shocked. David had never told me what to do before. This didn't have the tone of a suggestion; it was a clear direction. *Was he trying to control my life?*

In prayer, Jesus told me to look back in my journals, and there in my own handwriting was the guidance to sell the house and donate the funds. I saw that I'd been trying to hold onto the last remnant of control I thought I had over my life, and all that David wanted for me was freedom.

I still had resistance to the idea of losing both my family and New Zealand. Regardless, I knew I had to follow through with the guidance. Being in integrity was essential and feeling split was simply painful. A week later I called Jackie and asked if she would help me sell the house. I shared the whole experience with her, and she was very supportive. When Roger got on the phone he began reflecting the doubts in my mind, asking if I was absolutely sure about my decision to sell the house. He started coming up with alternative options. The first was to sell half of the house to him so I would have it to come back to. The second was to sell the house and invest in his company, leaving me some back up finances. The more Roger came up with plans C, D, and E, the easier it became for me to see that plan A— the Spirit's plan—was all I truly desired.

Not long after making the decision to sell the house, friends in Australia wrote expressing their desire to start a spiritual community. For the first time, I felt free from being drawn to a location because of family ties. I was able to pray to the Spirit, to be shown clearly where David and I were to go, and what was to unfold next. Perhaps we would travel forever. I felt open to anything.

Following Through

> "The teacher of God is generous out of Self interest. This does not refer, however, to the self of which the world speaks. The teacher of God does not want anything he cannot give away, because he realizes it would be valueless to him by definition. What would he want it for? He could only lose because of it. ... But he does want to keep for himself all things that are of God, and therefore for His Son. These are the things that belong to him. These he can give away in true generosity, protecting them forever for himself." M-4.VII.2

Shortly after listing my house for sale, Jackie emailed to say that I had a buyer offering the full asking price. Feeling anxious, I sat with the doubts that immediately arose. It was the familiar squeeze of approaching the eye of the needle: What if this isn't my calling? What if David goes off with another partner and I am left with no money of my own and nowhere else to go? How do I really know this is the Spirit's plan? Remaining in prayer over the following days, I trusted the outcome to the Spirit and the house was sold within a week.

David was now traveling in Europe for several weeks, so it was up to me to transfer the funds to the ministry. It felt like going into the unknown, which was very inspiring because I knew my only purpose was mysticism.

Slowly and prayerfully following through with each practical action, I allowed the waves of doubts to arise and be released with each step. I continuously remembered that it was the Spirit's guidance that I was following. Everything flowed effortlessly, and once the transfer was complete, I felt that nothing had really changed. Nothing except that I was no longer dealing with anxiety and guilt. So, in fact, everything had changed!

It was another experience of seeing that the fear of sacrifice and loss is a buildup of tension that heightens before it is released from the mind. I really believed that I would lose something—my freedom, my choices, my independence. But in following the guidance to give over what I was holding onto, I gained my freedom and was released from the belief that I could make the wrong choice. I'd also realized once again that I did not want to be independent from God. I felt trust return, along with the remembrance of who was in charge of the plan of awakening. I remembered how anxious I had been when I had personal money; I worried that I could misuse it. Now I felt completely free—money and stewardship were finally in the hands of the Spirit, as was I!

Chapter Twenty-Seven

I Am Home

Summer 2007

"And now in all your doings be you blessed.
God turns to you for help to save the world.
Teacher of God, His thanks He offers you,
And all the world stands silent in the grace
You bring from Him. You are the Son He loves,
And it is given you to be the means
Through which His Voice is heard around the world,
To close all things of time; to end the sight
Of all things visible; and to undo
All things that change. Through you is ushered in
A world unseen, unheard, yet truly there.
Holy are you, and in your light the world
Reflects your holiness, for you are not
Alone and friendless. I give thanks for you,
And join your efforts on behalf of God,
Knowing they are on my behalf as well,
And for all those who walk to God with me."

AMEN M-29.8

A Merge Is Occurring

I had observed during gatherings that David sometimes spoke directly as the Spirit and at other times as "David." Regardless, the presence was consistent; the same light and clarity of the Spirit shone through his being and his words. The faces in the audience lit up in recognition of the truth; they felt such a strong connection, regardless of who they perceived David to be—a friend they could relate to, or the Voice for God.

As for me, much of my journey had involved two aspects of myself—the questioner and the Spirit. Now, however, I could feel a merge happening within my mind. The Holy Spirit no longer felt like a separate source that I prayed to. It was more of a quiet awareness of truth, an ever-present answer to whatever was arising.

This morning I felt a surge of inspirational energy and felt the prompt to sit and write. This writing felt like a culmination of everything I had learnt over the past two years, and it came directly from the Voice of the Spirit that I am:

The truth is true and only the truth is true. This profoundly simple state-ment, when applied to every seeming problem, has the power to bring the mind out of confusion and fear, and back into the simplicity and safety of the present moment, in an instant. But what is the truth?

Jesus said, "I am the way, the truth and the life." The truth is an experience that God Is; it is a state of mind far beyond form. Words can be reflective of it, and point towards it, but the truth can be known only as an actual experience.

When Jesus said, "be as little children," he was speaking of an open state of mind, a willing and humble attitude that has happily released the belief that it knows what the world is for, and how it should be.

Remember this world is a substitute for Heaven. It is not your home. All memories, thoughts, relationships, places, events, and people are to be used for the glorious purpose of awakening. Tread lightly amongst the images. With grati-tude, allow them to be released from your mind. Only through true forgiveness can the mind be freed from illusions, and free, to accept reality as it was created by God the Father.

The name of God is the replacement for all separate purposes and meanings, and calls forth the remembrance that creation has one name, one meaning, and a single source that unifies all things within Itself. This is true forgiveness, and it leads to unified perception, which does not see separation and fragmenta-tion. This is the Love of God, which is not of this world. Do not waste another precious moment searching for meaning in images. The world is the past; it is over and done with.

Come, abide with me, trust in me, release the past, and give yourself to me in this holy instant. There is no alternative but to accept God's plan for salvation. To attempt another way is nothing but a distraction; meaningless in eternity, but tragic in time because of the unnecessarily conflicted state of mind that is being chosen. You have cause for freedom now. You have cause for happiness now. Acceptance is all that is required. Come and rejoice with me in the simplicity of the truth!

Spiritual Community Blossoms

As David and I were praying about what was coming next, I realized that my journey into mysticism would be a constant going into the unknown; beyond what I believed was possible. I now knew that this life was my path, the answer to my prayer for healing, and not something that was happening *to* me. I was finally experiencing that my will and God's Will were indeed one.

The next step of the Spirit's plan began to be revealed when friends who had followed our journey over the Internet felt prompted to join us in community. People from Canada, Europe, New Zealand, Australia, and the U.S., expressed their desire to come to the Peace House. Some wanted to come for retreats, and others felt to rent or buy houses in our street. They felt "called" as I had done, years before, to be of service and deepen in their relationship with God.

The collaborative nature of holy relationship was ready to expand far beyond "two." Each gift I had received and practiced with David—forgiveness, full communication, trust, patience, open-mindedness, and flexibility—were now gifts to be happily shared.

David was joyfully open-minded and receptive to every possibility, as if he were Jesus at the gates of Heaven, with arms open, saying, "Come! You're so welcome!" He knew that Jesus was in charge of the plan, and that everything would be provided—from housing to food to projects for everyone. Whilst the form of how things would look was unknown, with the Spirit leading the way, we knew it would be an adventure!

Little did we know the magnitude of the plan that was unfolding, in which many of us would come to live together in spiritual community, shining the light and sharing the message of truth around the world for years to come!

Remembrance of the Song

My journey with David has taken me into the experience that I prayed for many years ago. I asked to know a love not of this world; to experience holy relationship. Although David and I are no longer marriage partners, our love has not ended and is beyond the world of form. It is of God—its sole purpose is clarity of mind, happiness and freedom.

David continues to be a source of inspiration and support to me in an ever-deepening journey into mysticism. As I pause and reflect on the nature of our relationship, my heart fills with gratitude and I am moved to tears. No matter what the experience, David is always right here with me, in person or in mind, with twinkling eyes, in full support, knowing exactly what I am experiencing.

The spiritual journey of undoing and healing is a path of releasing fear based limits and accepting the opportunities the Spirit offers the heart. After saying "yes" to what is given, and "yes" to letting go many, many times—a forgotten song is remembered. It is the ancient song of a love and a home that cannot be found in this world. It is a prayer that never ceases—a simultaneous giving and receiving of gratitude. If this silent prayer had words, they would be, "How can I share Your Love?" The answer is always a blessing.

Extending the awareness of truth is the purpose of life. It is all I have and all I am. Everything has led to this state of mind—this total union with God.

The End—The Beginning

Glossary of Terms

David Hoffmeister, American mystic: David's journey involved the study of many pathways culminating in a deeply committed practical application of *A Course in Miracles*. In David's early life, he was shy and introverted. As he opened to a life of service, he underwent a total transformation of consciousness. The shy personality completely disappeared, and was replaced by a joyful, open, and loving expression. David's life is a living demonstration of the awakened mind. He has touched the lives of thousands with his consistently peaceful state of mind, radiant joy, and dedication to truth. He is a modern-day mystic and non-dual teacher who has been invited to over forty countries to share the message of love, oneness, and freedom.

A Course in Miracles (**ACIM**): ACIM is a complete, spiritual mind training tool that teaches the way to love and inner peace through forgiveness. The perennial wisdom of ACIM underlies all non-dual spiritual teachings. Through applying the teachings in daily life, one's thought system is reversed from the ego's, fear-based thinking, to a thought system based on love. The Course teaches discernment between illusions and truth, fear and love, the ego and the Holy Spirit. It is also a transformational meditation program and it uses relationships as a means for practicing forgiveness, and learning how to be of true service beyond the perception of suffering. It is a pathway of deepening in devotion to Christ, which is our true Identity. The Course contains a 365 Lesson Workbook, a comprehensive Text, and a Manual for Teachers. It has supplementary booklets on the topics of Psychotherapy, Prayer, Forgiveness, and Healing. ACIM was initially scribed (channeled) and edited during the years of 1965–1972 by two psychology professors at Columbia University in answer to a prayer.

Metaphysics: Beyond physics, or beyond the physical. The guiding principles and purpose of all non-dual spiritual teachings are to take the mind from identification as an individual, personal self to the awareness of our spiritual nature and reality. The metaphysics as taught in ACIM are that only love is real, therefore all else is a perception based upon the illusion of separation from God. Through forgiveness, all beliefs and perceptions of separateness and fear are released and replaced with love.

Cause and effect: The mind is causative and what is seen in the world of form is an effect. For example, the perception of sickness comes from the belief in sickness. True healing is at the level of mind, and can only be accomplished through forgiveness.

Mind training: The practice of aligning the mind with the Spirit and releasing ego thought patterns and beliefs. Mind training is essential to be able to be present and focussed, and therefore able to hear the Spirit's guidance, which releases the mind from fear-based thinking. *A Course in Miracles* and meditation are highly effective mind training tools.

Transfer of training: The Holy Spirit's thought system involves a retraining of the mind to a different perception of everyone and everything. The ACIM Workbook involves exercises to help generalize the Workbook Lessons, and learn how to make no exceptions. Practically speaking, this means applying the Workbook Lessons to all areas of one's life, and thought system, without exception. This practice is essential, for to make one exception is to block the awareness of the all-inclusive nature of true perception; there are no exceptions in love. This learning leads to unification, "... perception fuses into knowledge because perception has become so holy that its transfer to holiness is merely its natural extension." T-12.VI.6

Mind watching: Is the practice of observing the mind, where we learn to recognize the ego's thought patterns, and ask the Spirit for help in releasing them. Mind watching leads to an experience of being the "observer", and allows for the Voice for God—love-based intuition—to be heard.

Attack thoughts/doubt thoughts: Any thought that is not of love. They are judgmental thoughts that deny one's innocence and identification with the Spirit. These thoughts arise from the belief in separation, unworthiness, and lack of trust.

Holy Spirit: The small, still, voice within—the Voice for God. The Holy Spirit is the guiding light that is a reminder of innocence, safety, and forgiveness. Through a devoted practice of turning to this presence and following it, a merge occurs where we realize that the Holy Spirit is our own heart guiding us home.

Guidance: Directions from the Holy Spirit, which are always in alignment with awakening. The purpose of guidance is to heal the mind from its identification with the ego—the personality self. Specific guidance may come in the form of words, intuitive feelings, signs, and messages, and may come through external symbols, such as trusted companions. Guidance leads the mind into a consistent experience of oneness with God.

Projection/projecting: The attempt to get rid of what you do not want. Every upset about a person, oneself, or the world is projection and can only be released from the mind through forgiveness. The Spirit extends love and truth, and the ego projects, blames, and makes illusions/stories. To believe you can project onto a person, or situation, is to identify with the ego.

Separation: Is the belief that we have separated from our Source—from God—and that we can, and do, exist apart from him. The belief in separation engenders enormous guilt and fear, and a belief in lack. Identifying a sense of separation from God is at the root of all healing; be it physical, emotional, or spiritual. All attempts to fill a sense of lack through worldly means, such as love and approval from others, money and possessions, or self-improvement, ultimately fail. Our only true need is direct connection with our Source, being the love that we are. All worldly relationships and "problems," reflect this core belief that we are a separate self, and in this way they present an opportunity for forgiveness, which leads to the experience that we are not separate from God, from love.

Purpose:
1. The ego's purpose involves improving and maintaining a personality self and an autonomous life within the world. It therefore uses the body for pride, pleasure, and attack. Because its purpose is the denial of one's identity as the Spirit, it is without a real purpose.

2. The Holy Spirit's purpose is forgiveness—awakening to true freedom and joy. Desiring the Holy Spirit's purpose aligns the mind with inner listening. When motivation is based purely on following the Spirit's guidance, identification shifts from a separate self, to being the Spirit.

Private thoughts: The ego is the belief in a private mind with private thoughts. It is the way the ego attempts to hide and protect its thought system and maintain a sense of separation and guilt. Our true reality is oneness—communion with God—a state wholly without private minds and thoughts. The practice of exposing what we believe to be our *personal*, private thoughts for healing, is transformational. It brings an experience of the truth—which is that private thoughts are of the ego. We experience that they are not "my real thoughts," and nor are they "mine alone"—there is simply one ego thought system. When brought to the light of truth, they literally dissolve away.

Mighty companions: Companions who share and support our purpose of awakening.

Mysticism: The purpose or goal of mysticism is to transcend limited identification, and become fully aware of oneness with God—the ultimate reality—through direct experience. Transformation of consciousness and full identification with the Spirit involves a devoted commitment to spiritual practices such as meditation and prayer. It also requires mind training through the study and practical application of a non-dual spiritual text such as *A Course in Miracles*.

Mystic: One whose life is devoted to knowing one's true identity as the Spirit, and to abiding in the living experience of God. A mystic knows there are no short-cuts on the journey of transformation, and will speak of the devotion, strength of mind, and single-pointed desire that are required to overcome the ego entirely. A mystic has found an inner contentment, a peaceful joy that is deeply attractive, fulfilling, and total, and therefore has no worldly goals.

True and false empathy: False empathy is attempting to heal, fix, or change a person or problem in the world while still believing that the problem is real. True empathy is identification with the Spirit, which is a state of mind that does not understand or believe in suffering, and can therefore be truly helpful and effective.

Special relationship: A relationship where a special someone, or something, is expected to meet the needs of making you feel *happy*, *safe*, and *secure*. In truth, only God can be the source of happiness, safety and security. In this way, all special relationships involve expectations that cannot be met and therefore these relationships maintain guilt, and involve compromise, resentment, and fear.

Holy relationship: When a special relationship is given over to the Holy Spirit, it is used for undoing the ego, which leads to true joy, and collaboration. In this way, holy relationship is *purpose*. Rather than being used to maintain and improve one's self-concept, the purpose of holy relationship is to release the identification from ego-based roles, and align the mind with a deeper commitment and certainty. The basis of holy relationship is the understanding that there are no real differences possible in unified awareness—in heaven or reality. Love is all-inclusive because love *is* one. The result of a deep commitment to holy relationship is freedom, and love, because what is being healed within this commitment is one's own relationship with God.

Learn More about Kirsten

Visit Kirsten.I-Am-One.net to stay connected with Kirsten Buxton. Find her tour dates and social media appearances, enjoy her free online talks and videos, subscribe to her blog, and relax with her music.

Also by Kirsten Buxton

Trust: Guided Meditation CD with David Hoffmeister
Music CDs: Quantum Love, Holiness, Strawberry Fields 2012 & 2013 Compilations.

Books by David Hoffmeister

Going Deeper
The Mystical Teachings of Jesus
Awakening through *A Course in Miracles*
Movie Watcher's Guide to Enlightenment
Quantum Forgiveness: Physics, Meet Jesus
Unwind Your Mind Back to God: Experiencing *A Course in Miracles*

Available in print, eBook, and audiobook formats. Select materials available in thirteen languages.

Living Miracles

Visit LivingMiracles.org to learn more about the Living Miracles Community, personal silent retreats, and to browse our online store.

More Resources for Awakening

NonDualityOnline.com Kirsten Buxton and David Hoffmeister are faculty members of the Tabula Rasa Mystery School, a 30-Day Residential immersion in the mind training of *A Course in Miracles*. Supported by ancient and present day non-dual teachings, this program is designed to lead you into an experience: it is an invitation to Know Thyself!

MiraclesHome.org Enjoy more intimate mind training parables with David Hoffmeister and his first students at the Peace House.

Awakening-Mind.org To learn more about David Hoffmeister, visit his non-profit Foundation devoted to teaching and learning forgiveness.

ACIM.biz Visit this portal website for links to many free resources, educational mind training support programs, and sites based on David Hoffmeister's Awakening Mind teaching.